Passive Annual Heat Storage

Improving the Design of Earth Shelters

- Revised 2013 -

John Hait

Published by:
Rocky Mountain Research Center (RMRC)
PO Box 1431
Chino Valley, AZ 86323, U.S.A.

For more information please visit: www.EarthShelters.com

Illustrations by: John Hait
Cover image by: Anton Reznikov

ISBN: 0615905889
ISBN-13: 978-0615905884

To Alice... no one could write a book without a very patient and loving wife, and to my sons, John, James, and Justin.

Contents

Acknowledgements

I would like to thank all of the individuals who have helped make this book possible:

Ron Preston, Mary Alto, Herb Carson, Tom & Sharon Lukomski, Helen Tabish, Steve Carlson, Kimberly Eldredge, and Mike Oehler.

I especially want to thank Ed Hawran for his years of hard work and dedication to the Rocky Mountain Research Center as well as my son, James Hait, who faithfully carries the torch.

Forward

This book is an innovative, yet practical, guide for the pioneer in Passive Annual Heat Storage. It is thirty years of proven science. It explains in detail the ultimate in year-round energy conservation. Without mechanical equipment or commercial power, Passive Annual Heat Storage (PAHS) inexpensively cools a home through blistering hot summers. It saves those precious BTUs, and then returns them automatically when they are needed to keep the home comfortable through frigid northern winters. Summer's excess heat is, of course, free solar energy. Non-mechanical YEAR-ROUND storage of this abundant natural resource is a whole new technology; its basic concepts, goals, and methods are substantially different from the passive solar heating with which most readers are familiar. This book presents these unique concepts, in a clear and easy-to-understand manner.

In order for such a science to grow, information must be gathered from the people who use it. Therefore, we invite you to apply the principles of Passive Annual Heat Storage in your own home designs without additional charge or license.

As you begin designing your own Passive Annual Heat Storage home, you will, no doubt, have a million questions... we all do. We expect a deluge of mail, so please read the whole book first, as your question may have already been answered. Some questions, though, can only be answered by further experience. If we all share our experiences we can all benefit. For all pioneers, as Sir Isaac Newton once observed, are "standing on the shoulders of giants."

In the past 30 some years, a number of PAHS homes have been built around the world. And everyone always asks, "Where can I see one?" The problem is that when one opens his house up to the public, the result is a deluge of people. At present, there are no homes I know of where the owners permit visits. I wish there were so I could direct you to them. However, their experience is universal.

PAHS is basically a simplified explanation of the laws of physics. So, if builders have followed the instructions herein, then they will do well.

But if they make heat-flow compromises, the performance will be diminished.

As you actually experiment with Passive Annual Heat Storage we would appreciate it if you would drop us a line detailing your design, how easily it went together, and how well it finally works. Such information will help us in preparing any future books so we can all advance together. After all, the field of solar technology is not an old and mature science as some would have us believe, but a pan of hot buttered popcorn... you never know what may pop out next!

You may contact us through our website at www.EarthShelters.com

Chapter 1 – Improving the Earth Shelter

COOL
MOIST

WARM
&
DRY

The control of underground heat-flow is a steadily expanding technology. Considerable advancement has now been made toward the production of COLD-CLIMATE homes that require no mechanical heating or cooling whatsoever. By using a revolutionary process called *Passive Annual Heat Storage* (PAHS), heat can be collected, stored and retrieved over the entire year, without using energy robbing mechanical equipment.

Plain old dirt is the ideal heat-storage medium. Heat is stored naturally in the earth as it soaks up the warm summer sunshine.

The earth retains this heat until cold weather arrives, then it slowly relinquishes its store to the open air. The summer-long heating up and the winter-long cooling off produce a year-round constant temperature twenty feet into the earth. Interestingly, this constant temperature mirrors the average annual air temperature.

An earth sheltered home designed with the principles of Passive Annual Heat Storage, controls the summer heat input and winter heat loss to establish a new average annual inside air temperature, which in turn, will produce a new constant temperature in the earth around the home. The home and the earth will work together to remain within just a few degrees of this average all year long. In this way, the environment around the earth sheltered home can be acclimatized to any suitable temperature. Of course, a home set comfortably in a nearly constant 70°F (21°C) environment needs neither air conditioners nor furnaces.

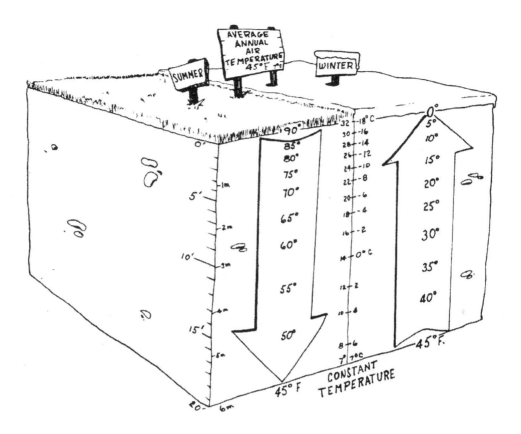

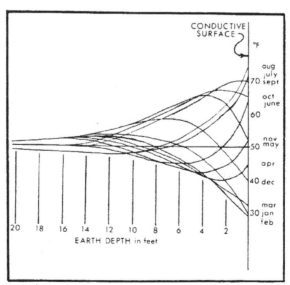

Figure 1 Monthly natural underground temperatures are averaged as they slowly soak into the soil from outdoors until, at about 20 feet deep, the whole year's temperature changes become a SINGLE AVERAGE.

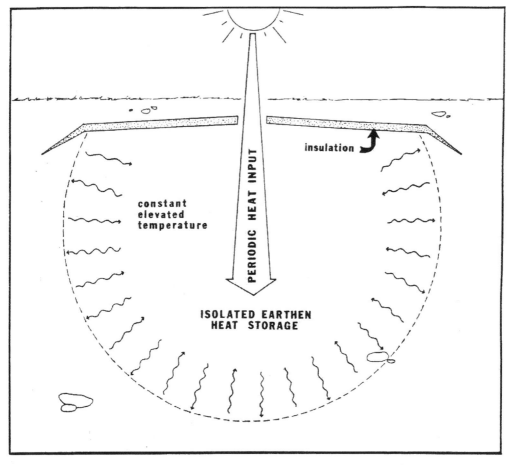

Figure 2 Thermal isolation of a large body of earth using an insulation umbrella. The umbrella eliminates encasing the whole thing in insulation.

The First Working Example

This unique heat control method was still in its infancy in January of 1981 when a major feature of Passive Annual Heat Storage, an Insulation/Watershed Umbrella, was incorporated into the design of an earth-sheltered home that was being built in Missoula, Montana USA. This home, called the Geodome, because of its shape, has its Insulation/Watershed Umbrella extended into the earth about 10 feet (3 meters) beyond the walls of the house, and encloses a two-foot (.6-meter) deep portion of earth on the roof. (Figure 4)

The building is monitored by 48 temperature and 5 moisture sensors. By the autumn of 1981, the temperature 10 feet (3 meters)

Figure 3 The Geodome in Missoula, Montana, USA. The first working example of Passive Annual Heat Storage.

under the surface, 12 feet (3.7 meters) behind the north wall, and 2 feet (0.6 meters) beyond the insulation itself, had been heated by excess summer heat from its usual 45°F to 64°F (7-18°C). The two-foot (0.6 meter) deep portion of insulated earth on the roof was warmed up to 77°F (25°C), while two feet under the floor it was 68°F (20°C). Throughout the first year, the north wall temperature on the second floor of the home varied only 6 degree, from a high of 72°F (22°C) in September to a low of 66°F (19°C) the next February. Thus the home has been snugly wrapped with a nearly 70°F (21°C) layer of earth, several feet thick (1 meter), which has kept the home comfortable all winter. Even though the insulation umbrella is only half as big as we now know it should be, the earth around the home remains warm and dry!

This outstanding performance has provided operational proof of the advantages of Passive Annual Heat Storage over conventional earth shelter design methods. As a result, further improvement has been made in the art of long-term-heat-storing.

Improving the Earth Shelter

Earth sheltered homes do enable the non-mechanical methods of passive solar heating to be used more effectively, because earth sheltering is inherently energy efficient. Some solar-heated earth-sheltered homes have worked quite well in selected climates. Even the better ones have been able to maintain a fairly stable temperature for only a week or so in inclement weather without needing back-up heat. Generally, passive-solar homes of all types have been able to collect only a portion of their space-heating needs because of one inherent problem: Solar energy simply isn't there when it is needed.

The noon sun is highest in the sky on June 21st, and lowest at the tail-end of December. It provides plenty of heat in the summer, but thanks to short days and foul weather, heat availability all but disappears in the winter, especially in the cold and cloudy Northwest. So, attempting to collect a home's heating needs in the winter-time is like trying to collect milk from a dry cow!

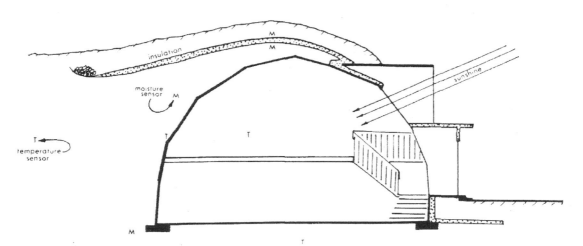

Figure 4 The Geodome cross-section showing the first, although small, insulation/watershed umbrella. Also shows the locations of the important temperature and moisture sensors.

What is needed to bring solar heating out of the dark ages is an inexpensive method for storing large quantities of heat over the entire year in a simple, natural, passively-operated reservoir: the earth. However, conventional earth-shelter designs do not take full advantage of the fine heat-storing ability (thermal mass) of the earth. A simple heat flow principle tells us why: Heat flows by conduction from warm places to cool places.

Conventional earth-sheltered homes prevent the earth around them from getting warm enough in the summertime to allow the heat to flow back into the home in the wintertime. While the concrete may warm up to room temperature, the earth around the building usually has its heat flow characteristics dominated by the colder outdoor weather conditions, rather than the controlled indoor temperatures. This occurs because the heat-storing earth is usually insulated from the heat-collecting house and not insulated from the generally cooler out-of-doors. Therefore the conventional insulation layout actually prevents the home's average annual air temperature from establishing a sufficiently warm, deep-earth constant temperature.

Storing a large amount of heat at room temperature requires a large amount of thermal mass. The relatively small warm storage mass of the conventional solar-heated earth-sheltered home, prevents the use of the abundant summer heat. Heat can be stored to last for only a week or so in cloudy winter weather before a back-up heater must be turned on. Homes that are restricted by small thermal storage are thus forced to resort to winter-oriented passive solar heating, which discards the energy-rich summer sunshine by shading. This also limits building locations to those where sunshine is readily available in the wintertime.

For an earth sheltered home to remain warm all winter from heat gathered six months earlier, the heat-storing earth must be kept both warm and dry. When cold rain water is allowed to soak into the ground around the building, as in conventional earth sheltering, it not only causes waterproofing difficulties, but it cools off the earth.

Further improvement is also needed in the current methods of supplying fresh air to tight underground structures. Most ventilation methods bring in hot air during the summer and cold air all winter.

Recognizing such problems is the first step toward solving them. Now, all of these problems can be solved by using the principles of Passive Annual Heat Storage.

How Passive Annual Heat Storage Works

Passive Annual Heat Storage is a proven process allowing summer's heat to be absorbed out of the home, keeping it cool and comfortable, storing this heat at room temperature in the dry earth around the building for conduction back into the home.

This reserve can then be conducted into the home anytime the indoor temperature attempts to fall, even through an entire winter. The home and earth together will maintain their comfortable temperature automatically, within just a few degrees.

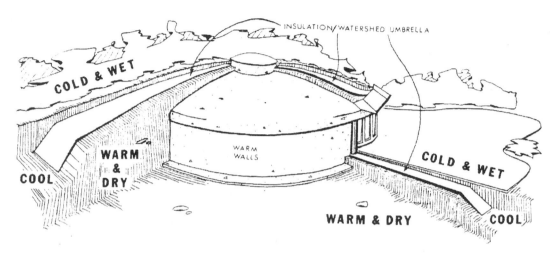

Figure 5 An INSULATION/WATERSHED UMBRELLA on an earth-sheltered home isolates a large body of earth that will have its constant temperature raised to a comfortable level.

This unique method for maintaining a deep-earth constant temperature of about 70°F (21°C) is based on several fundamental principles of physics:

1. Heat flows by conduction from warm places to cool places, and will ONLY return when the original source cools to a temperature which is below the storage temperature.
2. Far more solar heat is available in the summertime than in the wintertime.
3. Earth is an ideal thermal mass for storing heat over time periods well in excess of 6 months.
4. The constant temperature 20 feet (6 meters) into the earth is a reflection of the average annual air temperature.
5. It takes six months to conduct heat 20 feet (6 meters) through the earth.

Earth shelter technology can be significantly improved by a

balanced application of these simple principles. Passive Annual Heat Storage overcomes the deficiencies of conventional earth-shelter and passive-solar design by isolating a large thermal mass of dry earth around the home with a large Insulation/Watershed Umbrella, so that the earth itself may be warmed up to room temperature (Figure 5). To contain this heat we must cause the heat to flow between the earth and the home, rather than the earth and the out-of-doors. Therefore, all short conductive paths to the outdoors must be cut off. The insulation need not enclose all of the earth underneath and to the sides of the home because heat which flows 20 feet, or more, through the earth will be delayed long enough so that warm summer weather will arrive before last year's heat can make it all the way out from under the umbrella.

The home will establish its own average annual air temperature by controlling the summer heat input and the winter heat loss. Therefore it will now produce a new deep-earth (20 feet or more) constant temperature all the way around the home. Since heat moving both in and out is under control, the home's operating temperature may be adjusted to any average temperature we wish.

The Insulation/Watershed Umbrella also keeps the entire earth environment around the home dry, preventing the heat in the earth from being washed away and making waterproofing a cinch.

Cost

Passive Annual Heat Storage, including the earth tube ventilating methods suggested in this book, are inherently INEXPENSIVE in comparison to the usual cost of building an earth-sheltered home. The Insulation/Watershed Umbrella is made by laminating layers of rigid insulation with at least three layers of polyethylene sheeting. It is long lasting and relatively inexpensive to buy and install. Only a little more insulation is needed than with conventional methods of putting insulation on an underground home, since the subterranean surfaces will be left un-insulated. Also, waterproofing costs are reduced considerably because the home sets in a dry environment.

A little insulation, a little plastic, a little pipe and a whole lot of thought about how they should be installed, makes Passive Annual Heat Storage the least expensive energy management system anywhere.

Read on! The principles described in this book will greatly enhance the operation of any earth-bermed or earth-sheltered structure, and with a little design finesse, ANY STRUCTURE.

The rapidly advancing science of underground heat flow has opened the door to a whole new array of home design methods that will make heaters and air conditioners to homes what paint is to a beautiful stone wall!

Chapter 2 – Passive Annual Heat Storage

Developing Passive Annual Heat Storage
– An Illustration

Baked dry in August, frozen stiff all winter; a Montana sod buster and his neighbors battled the elements. They shivered through the frigid northern winters, gathering buffalo chips for fuel to ward off the frostbite.

Our field farming friend noticed that the vegetables in his root cellar never got hot and never got cold. They were always comfortable. He wasn't! So he installed a window in his root cellar and moved in.

Within the first year the unheated indoor temperature rose from its natural 45°F (7°C) to 55°F (13°C), all by itself. This drastically reduced the amount of fuel he needed, but his neighbors just laughed at him and continued gathering buffalo chips.

This rise in temperature was a surprise improvement since everyone had told him that it would always be 45°F (7°C) no matter what. Mulling this over in his mind he thought: "If I could only raise the temperature another 10°F or 15°F (6 or 8°C) I wouldn't need any buffalo chips at all!"

But how can you intentionally raise the constant temperature that occurs naturally in the earth? Well, he had already raised that average temperature about ten degrees by installing the window. He reasoned, "It must be like raising the natural level of a lake. You let more water in AND less water out. That's it!"

He grabbed his hat and dashed into town. Soon he returned with a pickup load of Styrofoam insulation and several rolls of plastic sheeting. He put the insulation and plastic over the top of his home, dirt and all, and covered the whole thing with another layer of earth.

All summer long, the heat which collected inside soaked into the ground to keep his home cool and comfortable. Just as he had suspected, the newly insulated earth began warming up from 55°F to 65°F (13° to 18°C) and, finally by fall, all the way up to 71°F (22°C). When cold weather arrived, the earth remained warm and kept his new earth sheltered abode cozy all winter. Our subterranean sod buster was at last continuously comfortable. He had invented PASSIVE ANNUAL HEAT STORAGE!

And his neighbors? Well, times have changed. Now a big monopoly collects and distributes all the buffalo chips and goes to the Public Service Commission each month to ask for another rate hike.

The Ultimate Improvement

An ultimate energy conservation system should:

1. Be simple and straight forward.
2. Work on the natural annual heat cycle.
3. Collect and store free heat whenever it is available.
4. Automatically bring the heat out of storage when needed.
5. Provide ALL of a home's heating and cooling needs.
6. Provide a continuous supply of fresh air.
7. Provide a surplus of energy of other needs.
8. Not use mechanical equipment.
9. Never break down or wear out.
10. Work in climates all over the world.
11. Be inexpensive and easy to build.

The ultimate improvement in energy-efficient building design is Passive Annual Heat Storage. How much more of an improvement can be made?

This ultimate energy conservation process is surprisingly simple: the sun heats the house, and the house heats the earth. When the sun isn't out, the earth heats the house. Although the physics of underground heat flow is complex, Passive Annual Heat Storage can be easily applied by knowing a few easy-to-understand principles.

How well we understand the way things work determines how well the houses we design will work. We must also know how things do not work, since a design based on erroneous assumptions will not work, or at best, will not work well.

How Heat Moves Around by Conduction

Underground heat flow is conductive; it naturally flows from warm places to cool places. Conduction has certain attributes that we must not confuse with other ways of moving heat around. It is unaffected by gravity: it doesn't "rise" as it does in fluids, such as water or air. Conducted heat doesn't always go in a straight line like radiant solar energy. Where it goes depends only on the temperatures involved and the kind of material the heat is going through. The rate of flow depends on how warm it is where it's coming from and how cool it is where it's going to. Its speed also depends on the amount of opposition it gets during the trip.

Insulation slows heat down and tends to keep it warmer on one side than the other. The amount of thermal resistance is expressed with a numerical value called "R" which describes the amount of thermal resistance, under standard conditions, through one-inch (2.5-centimeters) thickness of material. You'll usually find this R-value stamped right on commercial insulation but this value usually refers to the thermal resistance of the entire thickness of material. In this book I will generally use "R-value" to mean the entire thermal resistance rather than its value per inch.

Natural materials like earth also have thermal resistance. As with insulation, the R-value of a material accumulates with the distance the heat must travel through it. Two inches (5 centimeters) of a material slows heat down at least twice as much as a single inch (2.5 centimeters). Different materials with different R-values will have different resistances. Most texts that give the R-values for natural materials give them in "R" per FOOT (30.48 centimeters), a fact that can become confusing if one does not watch closely. (R/foot = 12R/inch)

Conductance is the opposite of resistance (K = 1/R). A substance like aluminum that conducts heat well offers very little resistance. A substance like fiberglass insulation that is a good heat resister is and therefore a poor heat conductor. Many substances are not really good conductors or resistors of heat flow. They could be called "semiconductors." Earth is one of these, yet the resistance it does have accumulates along the heat-flow path through the earth.

When heat is moving inside of a substance, it moves in a three dimensional fashion taking the path of least resistance. If it encounters an insulator, it is slowed down. But if a conductor (such as earth) is wrapped around the end of an insulator, such as a piece of Styrofoam, the heat will flow AROUND the insulation. It will be resisted only by the small cumulative resistance through the conductor. (Figure 6) Strategically placed insulation can therefore be used to force heat flow paths in the soil between the home and the earth's surface to become longer, creating the same effect as if commercial insulation had been put all the way around the home.

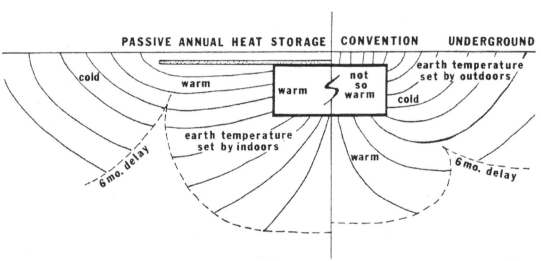

Figure 6 Underground heat flow paths both with and without Passive Annual Heat Storage. Long heat-flow paths are necessary for storage and retrieval of heat at room temperature.

All of the heat that flows from an underground house is not confined to the area up close to the horizontal layer of insulation (see left side of Figure 6). Rather, it has many paths that follow a parallel-like pattern as the heat seeks the path of least resistance around the insulation. This parallel-like movement occurs because adjacent points in the earth have the same temperature, and therefore, the heat at each point must flow parallel to the other, toward the cooler earth. Inserting the insulation also forces the lower-level heat-flow paths deeper into the earth making them even longer. This lengthening of the heat-flow paths has the same thermal effect as making the earth on the roof much thicker or sinking the whole house deeper into the earth.

The three dimensional heat-flow pattern and the R-value are not the only factors that determine how heat gets from one place to another via conduction. Heat storage is another property that substances like earth have; an ability that makes Passive Annual Heat Storage work.

Figure 7 If you don't like the weather, wait a few minutes! Weather is anything but static. Buildings should be designed by dynamic heat-flow methods.

Mathematically, the factors that determine how heat moves around by conduction can be expressed by a big and frightening formula that must be used millions of times over in detailed computer programs requiring extensive (and expensive) amounts of time to prepare. There are, however, some valuable principles that we may glean out of this formula so the average designer will never actually have to use or even remember it.

This complete conductive heat flow formula is:

$$Cp \; \rho \; \Delta T/\Delta \, t = (\Delta/\Delta x) \, (\Delta T/R\Delta x) \,) + (\Delta/y) \, (\Delta T/(R\Delta y) \,) + (\Delta/\Delta z) \, (\Delta T/R\Delta z) \,)$$

It is called the "dynamic heat flow formula", because it takes into account continuous changes that occur, rather than assuming that everything is always the same.

The heat flow formula which is most familiar to engineers is: $Q = (1/R) \; A\Delta T$. It is called the steady state, static heat flow or the heat loss formula. It has been extracted from the former one by ignoring some of its major factors. These very factors account for the earth's ability to store heat:

ρ = density

Cp = Specific heat

x,y,z = the three dimensions that make up the volume the heat is moving through.

t = time

What's left is a one dimensional formula that takes into account only:

A = surface area

T = Temperature

R = thermal resistance (R-value)

Q = Quantity of heat, usually BTU's per hour

Δ = "change in,"

For metric results, all factors must be metric—or 1 hr-ft2-/BTU-in = 8.065 hr-m2-o C/kcal-m

Underground heat flow is not simple, but this book will make it easy to use!

The thermal nature of a massive earth-sheltered structure makes it function very differently from the simplified, static or "steady state" heat-flow approximations that are customary in home design. In the past, designers have attempted to analyze earth shelters using only this steady state formula, because it is simple and easy to use. However, the factors from the dynamic heat-flow formula that have been ignored in the steady-state formula are the very ones that determine how a substance will store heat. They determine its "thermal mass" which is the ability to store heat proportional to the mass of the material being used. Light-weight materials used in conventional above-ground homes do not have very much thermal mass so they will not store very much heat. That is why the steady-state method could be used. Earth is heavy and will store tremendous amounts of heat. The way heat flows through the earth cannot be satisfactorily explained with the steady state method. Massive earth-sheltered homes must be designed using the principles of dynamic heat flow.

For many, dynamic heat flow constitutes a completely revised view of how heat moves. More importantly, it will improve the way we design homes, and in turn, the way they work.

This new view of subterranean heat flow goes beyond the traditional view of "earth as insulation" and includes more than the progressive view of earth as a temperature moderator. Because earth is a semiconductor that can store tremendous amounts of heat it can actually perform several heat-control functions.

Heat Flow in the Earth

There are three main properties of heat-conducting earth that make it useful for different heat control functions: thermal-resisting, heat-storing and temperature moderating. Beginning with resistance: What is the R-value of earth and why do text books disagree on its value? What actually causes it to change?

Compared to commercial insulations, earth is more of a conductor than an insulator. Under conditions that stay the same all the time it's often assumed to have an "R-value" in the neighborhood of .08 per inch (0.65 per centimeter) in comparison to many commercial insulations that range from 1 to over 7 per inch (8.06 per centimeter to 56.45 per centimeter) thickness. But the working R-value of earth will actually wobble all over the place. It isn't the basic composition that affects it so much as it is the amount of water present. It can drop from 0.4 per inch to 0.04 per inch (3.23 per centimeter to 0.32 per centimeter) in the middle of a big rain storm. This wide resistance fluctuation accounts for the discrepancy between different texts on what the R-value of earth really is. The obvious conclusion is: the thermal resistance of the earth can be regulated by controlling the amount of water present. Without such regulation the earth's resistance is actually out of control.

Underground water control, not just waterproofing, is extremely important, so, I have included two whole chapters on it.

It is often said, "The earth is a good insulator therefore you only need a small amount of it." OR, "Earth is a lousy insulator therefore commercial insulation must be used." As we have seen, neither of these statements is correct! Earth is generally about mid-range in thermal resistance in comparison with other materials. It has the qualities of an insulator and also of a conductor. To say that earth is a "lousy insulator" implies that it is not a useful material for heat control, and, therefore, should rightly be replaced by a man-made insulation.

Earth kept dry under the Insulation/Watershed Umbrella will actually keep stored heat close to the building for later use because this controlled R-value quickly accumulates along the heat-flow path. (Figures 3 and 5) Whenever heat must flow at least 20 feet (6 meters) through the earth, 95% of all heat flowing from an underground home will be stopped.

Used properly, earth is a superior heat-controller. Yet, it is generally quite impractical to have 20 feet (6 meters) of it on top of a house. On the roof, commercial insulation will give us the thermal isolation necessary for keeping the heat in and the cold out.

How effectively light-weight insulation can be used to reduce heat loss depends on how warm it is on one side and how cool it is on the other. If this temperature differential can be reduced then the total heat loss will likewise be reduced. Earth's ability to store heat produces a notable effect called temperature moderation that will substantially reduce this temperature differential.

Temperature Moderation

Weather conditions are anything but static. The thermal storage mass will be very effective in moderating these dynamic temperature changes even within just a few inches of earth.

Moderation takes place when a substance STORES heat because it takes a long time for each inch to heat up (or cool off) before the second inch is affected. It's like filling up an ice cube tray with water starting from one end. Each space must first fill before it overflows into the next, and so on. The time delay that occurs, because of the heat-storing and releasing process, is much longer than the time it takes for the weather to change. These ever-changing outdoor temperatures soon become muddled into a sea of previous temperature changes as they soak into the soil. The result is an average (moderation) of the temperature extremes that have occurred at the surface. (Figure 1)

Two feet (60 centimeters) of earth will completely average out a full day's worth of outdoor temperature fluctuations. Nighttime lows and daytime highs merge into a single, slowly-changing average, which is easier for the house to contend with than the extremes of the outdoor weather. Total heat flow through the roof of an earth-sheltered home, even with just 18 inches (46 centimeters) of earth on it, is substantially less than it would be with insulation alone (having an equivalent R-value) because of this moderation effect on the dynamic nature of weather conditions.

Earth's thermal properties are cumulative. That is, the greater the depth or longer the heat flow path, the greater the moderation effect. Seven to ten feet (2 to 3 meters) of earth will effectively isolate a subterranean surface from the vast majority of seasonal fluctuations.

A body of earth that is isolated from seasonal temperature changes may be used to store heat over many seasons. It may be used for Passive Annual Heat Storage.

Storing Heat in the Earth

Is the earth a big sponge, an unquenchable heat sink that always sucks heat away from an earth shelter, much the same way as an above-ground home when its heat blows away in the wind? (Only more slowly.) Static heat flow methods have led designers to believe just that. Their conclusion: The earth just outside the wall would always be 45°F (7°C) (in Montana), and heat loss would occur just as with the above-ground home, only at a slower rate. Therefore, the entire house must be insulated. Is that true?

No! Even the conventional earth shelter climatizes the earth around it to some extent. Passive Annual Heat Storage allows the newly climatized "floating temperature" to be ADJUSTED up to a comfortable year-round level!

Can stored heat actually be kept close enough to the home to be useful? Well, where does the heat flow as it leaves an earth shelter? Does it go down forever? No! If you dig deep enough the temperature is actually equal to or greater than that of the house.

Since heat only flows to where it is cooler it obviously will not go down forever. The depth where the temperature is naturally about 70°F (21°C) is quite deep, but at least we have established that it doesn't just go disappear into the earth.

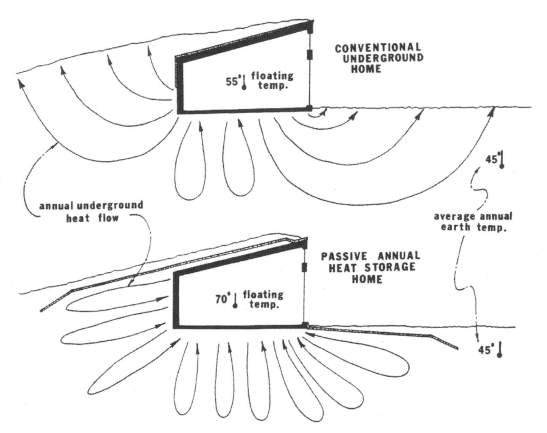

Figure 8 The "Floating Temperature" of a building is the basic average of temperature an earth-sheltered home will maintain if left unheated and without sunshine for a few weeks.

In the winter heat migrates upward because that is where the cold weather is. In the summer, heat flows down into the earth from the warm surface. If the path the heat must take is 20 feet (6 meters), or longer, three very interesting things happen:

The slow migration of heat into the earth takes about 6 months to reach the 20-foot (6-meter) mark. By then it's winter, and the surface is now colder than the deep-earth where the heat was headed, so it turns around and comes back out.

While the R-value of earth may be low, it nevertheless, does have an R-value. Given 20 feet (6 meters) of conductive path through the earth, this accumulated resistance and moderation effect will bring annual subterranean heat loss to a virtual standstill.

These effects occur wherever the path is very long, both from the walls horizontally and from the floor downward. Remember:

conduction doesn't care about gravity.

The warm temperature near the house does drop off gradually until it reaches the natural deep-earth temperature, 45°F (7°C) in Montana. But the distance the heat must travel is so long, and the temperature differences so slight, that total heat flow is essentially nil! The final result is the same as if a ball of earth 20 feet (6 meters) out in all directions had been dug up and had insulation wrapped all the way around it. Only it is far, far cheaper!

Since the heat that comes through the windows of a subterranean home may now be contained, it will be stored in and released from the earth for at least 20 feet (6 meters) by means of conduction. It is therefore, conduction-accessed heat storage. The working temperature of this conduction-accessed heat storage is controlled by adjusting the indoor average annual air temperature.

Average Annual Air Temperature

The actual temperature 20 feet (6 meters) down, without an earth-sheltered home around, is a reflection of the average annual air temperature. At that depth, a full year's worth of temperature changes have been moderated into a single, stable average. Likewise, the body of earth which we isolate to produce Passive Annual Heat Storage, will assume a new constant temperature that is a reflection of the artificial average annual air temperature we will produce inside the home.

If we adjust the average annual air temperature inside the home to be 70°F (21°C), then the deep-earth constant temperature will climatize itself to 70°F (21°C). This occurs NO MATTER WHAT THE OUTDOOR CLIMATE MAY BE! This kind of effect has been noticed even in conventional earth sheltered homes, though it occurs at a less-than-comfortable temperature.

If you speak to any earth-shelter owner, they will tell you that the house will "float" at some certain temperature, 50°F, 55°F (10°C, 13°C) or some other temperature. Since the deep-earth temperature, without a house in it, is say, 45°F (7°C) in Montana, why is it that the earth-sheltered home "floats" at some higher temperature? The existence of the home altered the deep-earth temperature. Therefore, the earth which surrounds the structure will actually become climatized to a new, nearly constant temperature: the "floating" temperature.

This view is proven out by both experience and computer simulations that have been conducted, such as the ones by the

Underground Space Center of the University of Minnesota. After a period of up to three years, these homes actually climatize the soil around them by absorbing heat into the earth until a new, long term, stable condition exists. At this point, their heating requirements flatten out and when left unattended and unheated, will actually "float" at a higher temperature than the same body of earth would maintain without the home in it. The home itself, because it is a solar collector, has actually modified the climate in the soil to produce a new thermal earth environment for the home to exist in. The trick is to design a home that will float at a comfortable temperature, such as 70°F (21°F C).

This same effect is what accounts for the recommendations in many of the more recent building design texts that only "perimeter insulation" need be used under the floor of a "slab-on-grade" home. The center of the floor is far enough from the outside that heat loss from this area is minimal.

Breathing Heat

This thermal storage ability allows excess heat from within the structure to be put away for later use. Since it is conducted into storage whenever the internal temperature attempts to climb, it is also conducted right back out whenever the home's air temperature attempts to fall, moderating the temperature of the AIR!

The earth environment actually breaths heat to and from the structure. Thus, the home and the heat-storing earth around it actually become a unified heat-flow system. Since such "breathing" occurs with even the slightest temperature change, the total heat flow system will maintain a temperature that varies only a few degrees all year. Unlike other solar-heated homes that are noted for their extreme temperature fluctuations through the day, a Passive Annual Heat Storage home's temperature change is barely perceptible even over several months!

Proper Passive Solar Heating

Annual heat storage requires a large amount of heat, a large amount of storage, and a large amount of time. Large masses soak up heat VERY SLOWLY and release it the same way. It is this very property that makes earth an ideal storage medium for the annual cycle. Conveniently, the heat's six-month time delay through a 20-foot (6-

meter) thickness of earth matches the time it takes this planet to go half way around the sun; the time period which determines our annual heating and cooling needs.

Yet most text books have not recommended high-mass houses; homes that have a very large thermal mass. It was believed that they would be difficult to heat or could never be heated. Certainly a large amount of storage will require the collection of a large amount of heat! Not by creating high temperatures for a few weeks in the winter, but by collecting heat over a very long time. This heat should be supplied at a MODERATE and comfortable temperature, to charge the entire thermal mass with heat over the entire cooling season. The "cooling season" is that portion of the year when ordinary homes are in need of cooling because of over-heating. This moderately warm heat that has been stored in the large thermal mass will then return to keep things warm all during the "heating season," that portion of the year when ordinary homes need to be heated.

Each of the four seasons has its own heat availability and its own heating requirements. Throughout the summer and early fall, an abundant supply of heat is readily available both in the form of solar radiation, called insolation, and warm air that enters through the doors and windows (and the earth tubes of Chapter 7).

These are items that are quite CONTROLLABLE. Unlike the "conventional passive approach", we actually WANT some of this heat to enter the home. Not all at once by using large directly south facing windows since that would only raise the air temperature to an uncomfortable level. The earth cannot soak up the heat that fast, so it is better to SPREAD IT OUT. Design the home for as EVEN a supply of this free outdoor heat as you can by using a more moderate amount of glass, not all facing south but with some to the east and west. Position the windows to maintain an indoor temperature 2°F OR 3°F DEGREES (1°C or 2°C) ABOVE THE AVERAGE ANNUAL AIR TEMPERATURE you wish to establish. Then a long wave of heat at just the right temperature will slowly lumber its way into the heat-saving earth. In actuality, the home is cooling ITSELF all this time and will maintain a delightful climate through blistering hot summers. The longer summer's heat is applied, the deeper into the earth it goes and the warmer the entire thermal mass becomes. Conversely, the longer the home must coast without heat, the deeper the heat must be retrieved from the earth, and the cooler the entire thermal mass will become.

In the fall, direct solar gain will be the dominate heat source. Outdoor air is no longer as warm and thus not available for extracting heat from. (Chapter 7 explains how to extract heat from warm air.) Yet a generous direct heat supply is still available. By now, some of the stored heat will have conducted its way back out of storage, especially at night and on cloudy days, whenever the temperature inside drops below the storage temperature.

In the winter, when the sun is low and days are short, and in many places, the sky is overcast; precious little solar heat is available. In such places, winter-oriented solar homes simply do not work. It's true that some heat is collected even on cloudy days, but compared to the amount available during the rest of the year it hardly warrants using over-sized windows and putting up with the accompanying large heat loss and wide temperature fluctuations. If, on the other hand, you've put away enough free summertime BTUs, you'll be comfy and warm ALL WINTER. Come spring, while others are moonlighting to pay their power bills, you can go fishing!

Underground temperatures are at their lowest in the spring-time but the sun returns then to give us a well-timed shot of free solar heat. In the spring, more heat is needed, so adjustable window shades should be wide open to collect as much sunshine as possible. Springtime heat will soak the deepest into the earth and will begin the long heat-storing

The Heat Storage Configuration (Figure 9)

Earth's well balanced traits such as heat storage, temperature moderation, thermal resistance, structural uses and low cost, make earth the most practical building material of all. Under-standing how it really functions will allow us to define the several different thermal jobs that the earth will accomplish, when we use it right. This will provide the pioneer with a suitable set of guidelines, starting points, basic sizes and configurations. These lay a fine foundation for the pioneering work in Passive Annual Heat Storage.

The different jobs that earth will perform for us depend on where it is in relation to the house, how it is insulated, the length of the conductive paths to the nearest surfaces and the average temperature it functions at. Three zones of heat-conducting earth can then be identified by their thermal functions. They are:
1. The Moderation Zone
2. The Isolation Zone
3. The Storage Zone

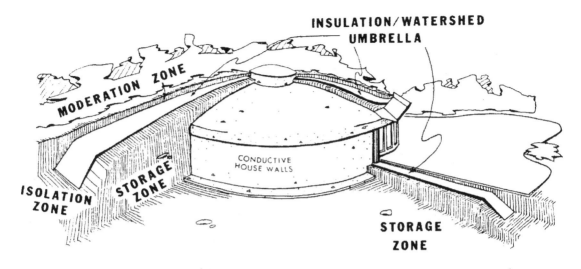

Figure 9 Three thermal zones are established by using an INSULATION/WATERSHED UMBRELLA. Each has its own job to do and each functions at a different average temperature: the MODERATION ZONE at the outdoor temperature; the STORAGE ZONE at the indoor temperature; and the ISOLATION ZONE which spans the difference between the indoor and outdoor temperatures.

THE MODERATION ZONE. The home and the earthen-heat storage area must be separated from the harsher weather outside. The insulation umbrella covers over the top of the house, its warm storage area and out seven to ten feet (2-3 meters) beyond it. A 2-foot (0.6-meter) layer of earth is put over the top of this insulation. Its purpose is to isolate the storage mass with a reasonable amount of temperature-moderating earth, support plant life, protect the insulation, and provide a permanent cover to protect the home. It functions in a wide temperature range that straddles the average annual OUTDOOR temperature.

This temperature-moderating function is the main one used in conventional earth sheltering and is called the Moderation Zone.

THE ISOLATION ZONE is a body of earth whose accumulated moderation effect and thermal resistance are sufficient for preventing appreciable heat loss from the structure AND its storage mass. It functions between the slowly changing seasonal average temperatures and the newly warmed deep-earth temperature. Its minimum of 7 to 10 feet (2 to 3 meters) of conductive path delays temperature changes so that the warm storage mass is affected only by a slowly changing average temperature. This ELIMINATES any need of wrapping the entire heat- storing body of earth with insulation. The isolation zone does just as its name implies; it isolates the inside temperature from the outside without using commercial insulation, except on the top where there is not enough earth for an effective isolation zone.

Figure 9 shows the relative positions of each of the three zones. The insulation is shaped like a large underground umbrella to aid its thermal operation and also to facilitate water drainage. The outer edges of this umbrella would generally be buried at least four or five feet below the surface. This defines a peripheral earthen mass which is the ISOLATION ZONE.

The actual temperatures in the isolation zone and the storage zone become muddled as the two merge together; exact distances are not as important as it is to understand the function of each zone. The 7- to 10-foot (2- to 3-meter) figure is a MINIMUM one, chosen from the studies undertaken by the University of Minnesota[1], and examined extensively in Chapter 5. In these studies, it is evident that 12 to 14 feet (3.7 to 2.4 meters) of isolation zone would be preferable in places around the home where there isn't room for a sizeable storage zone. However, all heat conductive paths from the warm home, through the earth, to the out-of-doors should never be any shorter than the 7 to 10 feet (2 to 3 meters) required for an effective isolation zone. Remember that conventional earth shelters are built with an isolation zone and a moderation zone. Lacking an effective warm storage zone, they have not been able to keep the earth warm enough so that heat could be conducted back into the home during extended cold, sunless periods. The temptation is to make the umbrella small thinking that the isolation zone is sufficient. It is not. The umbrella must also extend far enough to encompass a warm storage mass with an isolation zone around it too.

THE STORAGE ZONE is that body of earth which will be warmed to room temperature, so that the stored heat will conduct its way back into the home in the winter. When this storage mass finally becomes climatized, it will function at or near the desired interior temperature.

The storage zone is quite large. First of all, it includes that portion of earth which is on top of the roof and under the umbrella. Not all home designs will have the capability of supporting more weight than just the 2-foot (.6-meter) deep Moderation Zone. In that case, only the roof itself will store heat at room temperature. Secondly, it includes the warm earth to the sides, rear and front of the home, under the umbrella, out to within 7 to 10 feet (2 to 3 meters) of the uninsulated surface.

The largest body of earth available as warm storage zone is underneath the home. This earth is very well isolated from the outdoors and can be climatized for a great distance. Over a very long time the actual warm temperatures may extend 40 or more feet into the earth. However, the six-month delay through the first 20 feet (6 meters) prevents any of the heat that may be farther away from entering the home. It will maintain a very small temperature differential over very long conductive paths so that essentially no more heat will be lost into this very deep earth.

One limiting factor may be moving ground water. This water will carry the heat away and thus will limit the extent of deep-earth temperature modification. However, very few homes should be built very close to flowing ground water and water that comes down from the surface will be taken care of by the water-control methods discussed in the next two chapters.

A new thermal environment, UNDER THIS UMBRELLA, can now come into existence as the storage mass is climatized to achieve a new constant temperature. It and the home together, will maintain year-round within very narrow limits, on the order of 3°F to 5°F (2°C to 3°C) from the average.

The creation of an artificially warm environment surrounding a home is a completely new concept in home design. It provides us with a fresh viewpoint that changes what we expect buildings to do for us. In the past, a home was a container; it separated us from the elements. To make a home energy efficient, one would merely add enough insulation so that winter heat loss would be reduced to an acceptable minimum.

The task of keeping such a home warm or cool was given to machinery: furnaces and air conditioners. Never before was a home considered to be an adjustable environment that would, in itself, produce a continuously comfortable climate. A people-oriented environment, rather than just a shelter. It's the very first time you could have a home with a built-in temperature.

The Super-Insulated Situation

There is a dramatic difference between a Passive Annual Heat Storage home environment and the conventional or super-insulated above-ground house. All year long the above ground house has precisely the same outside surface area exposed to the harsh environment, regardless of the time of year. Unless you close off part of the house in the winter. This surface is designed to lose heat all winter, only at a slow rate because of the heavy amount of insulation.

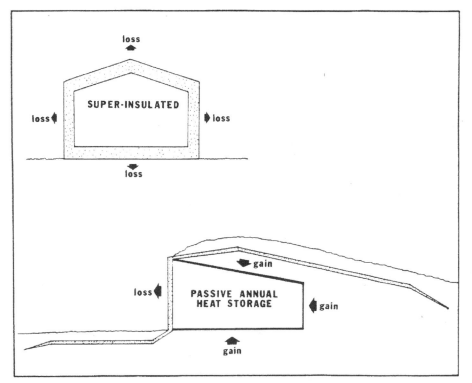

Figure 10 The super-insulated wintertime heat loser in comparison to the Passive Annual Heat Storage heat gainer. The heat-losing surface area has been drastically reduced because the new arrangement has stored its heat for later use.

The new subterranean environment, on the other hand, operates more like a south facing window. Although windows are known for their large heat losses, when the sun shines through them, even on a cold winter's day, they present a net HEAT GAIN to the inside. All winter long the subterranean surfaces of the improved earth shelter design are conducting heat back into the house, out of the storage mass. The walls, ceiling and floor provide a "heat gain" rather than a "heat loss." Therefore they act like a south facing window when the sun is shining. All but the exposed above-grade walls, which naturally should be designed using good energy conservation methods, are effectively REMOVED from the list of heat losers. Therefore only a fraction of the heat losing area remains, unlike the super-insulated house! A tiny heat losing area means that the home will actually have only a tiny total heat loss. Therefore, a Passive Annual Heat Storage home is far more energy efficient than any other cold-climate house.

This revolutionary concept produces a self-contained, self-regulating building which inherently provides for its entire thermal and ventilation needs, without the use of machinery or commercial energy sources. And it works throughout the ENTIRE YEAR, even in cold climates. Is that not truly a breakthrough?

However knowing all the intimate details of subterranean heat flow is merely an academic curiosity, unless it's all controllable. Old fashion underground houses had an earth environment that was really OUT OF CONTROL. The very first wandering heat grabber that must be harnessed is water, or all the other attempts at capturing that illusive animal (annual heat storage) will wash "down the drain."

Notes:

Chapter 3 – Why Water Washes Away The Heat

Water, water, water! What has a more dramatic influence on earth sheltering than water? Most underground homes are heavily laden with expensive waterproofing. Even then leaking problems persist. In most climates, the earth often remains moist long after the rain showers have passed. Water in the earth affects more than just the humidity and comfort of an earth shelter. The earth's R-value can drop 90% in a single rainstorm. In a matter of minutes, flowing water can rob heat that has taken months to be put in place by conduction.

A subterranean home placed in a DRY earth environment will function far better than the same home will in a wet one. The insulation/watershed umbrella will produce an artificially dry earth environment for your home fit into snugly. The reasons for this tremendous improvement become apparent as we take a close look at our wandering heat-grabber: water.

Water's Unique Properties

Water is a unique compound. Not only is it vital for life, but its thermal properties are outstanding among substances. Water stores heat and stores it very well. The amount of heat stored in any thermal mass, without counting a phase change, changing from ice to water, or water to steam and the like, is given by the formula:

Where Q = Quantity of heat stored (or removed)
 M = Mass
 Cp = Specific Heat
 T_1 = Starting Temperature
 T_2 = Final Temperature

(Note: its parts are contained in the large dynamic heat flow formula of Chapter 2.)

Mass (volume times density) is a significant factor in determining how much heat can be stored in a given substance. Generally the more of a substance we have, and the heavier it is, the more heat can be stored in it by raising its temperature.

For example, a cardboard box full of gold will store more heat than the same box full of dirt. A box full of air will not store anywhere near as much heat as a box full of dirt. Thanks to the air between the stones, a box of rocks will not store as much heat as that same box of dirt. However, a box full of inexpensive dirt will store just about the same amount of heat as a box full of solid concrete.

Figure 11 Each type of material will store a different amount of heat in cubic feet.

Water though, is unique. Thanks to its very high specific heat, the same box full of water can store about two and a half times as much heat as a box of dirt, but it weighs only about half as much! Water stores heat so well that it has become the standard by which all other substances are measured. Its specific heat is 1.

Many people have designed and used water heat storage systems, that have been made to work rather well. After all, the largest heat storage system in the world uses water. The oceans store such vast amounts of heat that they control the various climates of the entire planet. But have you ever tried to store water in a cardboard box? Containers, controls, piping, and pumps can make good thermal sense if done right. Unfortunately, they can cost enough that they might as well be a box of gold, especially if you expect to store heat for a whole year. Dirt on the other hand has two advantages over water, in spite of its lower specific heat; it doesn't leak and it's dirt cheap! Thus, earth sheltering is far more advantageous than any other heat storage method. However, if you have water in your dirt, you may also have trouble.

As mentioned above, a major change occurs in the thermal properties of any substance which soaks up water, because the thermal properties of water are so unusual. The R-value of a substance that has absorbed any water is just one of the variables that will vacillate depending upon the amount and stability of water. During a short rainstorm, the thermal resistance of the earth surrounding a subterranean home may fall from 0.4 to 0.04 per foot (3.2 to 0.32 per centimeter). If the R-value of earth can change dramatically when water is introduced. What do you suppose will happen to your insulation when it gets wet? If the insulation and the body of earth which surrounds the home can be KEPT DRY, the heat storage ability of the earth would be greatly enhanced and the integrity of the insulation maintained. So a large number of problems will be solved all at once by controlling the water rather than letting it run wild.

In addition to the wobbling R-value, there is another heat flow factor running rampant in the earth environment surrounding conventional earth shelters. Old fashioned underground homes have been plagued by this major problem, which has a simple solution. That solution is the Insulation/Watershed Umbrella. But first of all let's back up to see how an invisible concept has become obvious.

Transportive Heat Flow

How many types of heat flow are there? Three? Radiation, convection, and conduction, right? There's another one you probably haven't heard of: transportive heat flow. Put a tea kettle of water on the stove 'til it whistles. Now you've stored a fair amount of heat. Carry it into the parlor to make yourself a cup of instant java: TRANSPORTIVE HEAT FLOW!

Before you ash-can this noble volume and assign its author to the "coo-coo's nest," consider how the way we view the principles that make things work as we generally encounter them, affects the way we design things.

The purist will very quickly remind me that the action I have labeled "transportive heat flow," is in reality just convection; that is, a mass has moved from point A to point B and taken some quantity of heat with it. True! But ask anyone for a definition of convection and what will he say? "Hot air rises." Seldom do people remember that cool air must descend to allow the warmer air to rise, which is also an essential part of convective heat flow. They will go to elaborate means to provide a place for the hot air in their houses to go, and then forget to provide a place for the cool air to go. The result? Houses that have only two temperatures: too hot and too cold!

Natural convection takes place in other fluids too. I've seen too many mechanical solar heaters lose much of the heat they have gained right back out of their roof top collectors just because someone didn't remember any kind of heat flow except that which is powered by a pump!

The way we think of things has a direct bearing on the way we build things. Thinking of things in this new way will serve as a reminder so we will remember to design things in harmony with the way things really work. So let's carefully consider one of the major factors that affect the ability of an earth sheltered home to use the earth about it for heat storage: transportive heat flow.

All summer long, as I have described in chapters 1 and 2, heat from inside the home is absorbed by the earth, keeping the home refreshingly cool. If we can just hang on to that heat until winter, it will come back to keep us cozy all year. Then it rains. An inch (2.54 centimeters) of rain falling on the roof of a 1,600 square foot (149 square meter) home can amount to over 1,000 gallons (3785 liters)! That's over THREE TONS of water drenching the ground around your home, pouring through your heat storage bin! When all the upper surface of the storage zone is added to the 1,600 square feet you already have as a collecting bowl, one inch of rain adds up to (15,000 liters) almost 4,000 gallons! It hits the ground just a little above freezing, and oozes its way into your nice 70°F

(21°C) earth. Thermally, that earth is INSIDE your home because heat moves in and out through the walls and more than 20 feet (6 meters) of earth! When all this water heats up to room temperature, what happens? To protect the usual underground home from water in the conventional manner, there is probably a layer of gravel all the way up and over the roof and miles of drain tile to make sure the home stays dry. Right?

Oh, gravity drainage is so efficient!

Now you guessed it. All that stored heat gets washed RIGHT DOWN THE DRAIN!

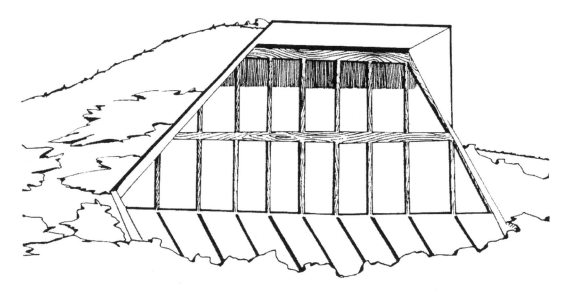

Figure 12 The John Means home, in Missoula, Montana USA. John recognized the problems that occur because uncontrolled water will wash away stored heat.

Tremendous amounts of stored heat that took months to be hidden away are being literally washed away by rain. The John Means home in Missoula, which was built a couple of years before the Geodome, experienced a noticeable temperature drop of 2°F or 3°F (1°C or 2°C) each time it rained, just like other conventional earth shelters do. Cool rain water flowed over the building and through the surrounding earth, warmed up from stored heat, and then drained away, taking the heat with it. The loss amounted to (conservatively) over 6.6 million BTU's per degree Fahrenheit (2.9 million kcal per degree Celsius) drop in temperature. Yet, the problem was amplified because the heat loss would be continual over a period of time roughly equal to the length of the storm. Only after drainage was complete could the 18 or more million BTU's (4.5 million kcal) be slowly replaced, only to have it rain again.

John designed his own home, and he did a fine job, using the best techniques available at that time. Won't you, while working on yours? Like all of us now in earth sheltering, he is a real pioneer. Remember what I said in the introduction about "standing on the shoulders of giants?" We have much to learn from everyone involved in this new science. John was perceptive enough to notice the way his home was working, and this rapid temperature drop was definitely caused by rainfall. No doubt the total loss was more than just 18 million BTU's (4.5 million kcal). However isolating any one cause is a notable achievement, since the effects of this solitary item are quickly muddled into a sea of variables.

Ordinarily, the slowly moving stored heat reduces the temperature differential in the earth from one inch to the next, to levels that are so small that what heat loss there is will continue being reduced to a trickle. So while this stored heat is in place, it acts as a barrier to rapid heat loss. Thus the overall thermal efficiency of an underground building is drastically reduced by the introduction of water into the earth about it.

More importantly, if we wish to have that heat RETURN to us in the winter, we MUST maintain its temperature ABOVE our desired average-annual-indoor-air temperature. Heat flows ONLY from warm places to the cool places. If we fail to keep our storage warm, no heat will return to us, unless we are willing to allow our winter indoor temperature to drop BELOW this rain cooled, uncomfortable storage temperature.

But why have designers permitted transportive heat flow to rob them of their greatest thermal tool? Again, how does the average person describe convection? Heat rises, right? Which way does the heat go when it rains through an unprotected earthen heat storage system? Ups and downs make a lot of difference to a designer, and few have time and money to become physicists too. The heat moved CONTRARY to the general expectation; it actually went down rather than up. Therefore, rain drenched earth is generally not recognized as a thermal problem at all, but only a waterproofing one.

Waterproofing on a building may keep it dry, or almost dry, with a river of water flowing over it, but the earth around the building will still be soaked. So, a new type of heat flow should be defined, even if only as a teaching aid: TRANSPORTIVE HEAT FLOW. To control our newly-defined heat flow type, we must merely control the water.

Chapter 4 – Water, Water, Everywhere – So Control It!

Comprehensive Water Control

Subterranean homes face a number of water control problems. Each source of water, each place where water is likely to show up, has its own characteristics that must be addressed if all water problems are to be solved. Not all moisture problems are caused by an excess of water either. Sometimes things may be too dry. This is also a water problem since we want to keep some things moist and other things dry. Thus all the water should be controlled.

The sources of water control problems include:
1. Rain water.
2. Stagnate surface water.
3. Running surface water.
4. Subsurface water on the roof.
5. Water flowing over the home.
6. Water flowing through the earth around the home.
7. Water in the drainage system.
8. Natural ground water, the aquifer, the water table.
9. Moisture in the soil.
10. Indoor moisture producers; bathrooms, kitchens, hot tubs.
11. Plumbing.

Uncontrolled water can cause these major problems:
1. Erosion.
2. Desert or swamp-like surface conditions.
3. Structural failure
4. Waterproofing failure, dampness, dripping, or flowing water inside the home.
5. Clogging of underground drainage systems.
6. Mold, mildew and insect invasion.
7. Flooding and drains that back up.
8. Overly dry or overly humid interiors.
9. TRANSPORTIVE LOSS OF VALUABLE HEAT and failure to achieve annual heat storage.

So, practical water control cannot be handled by mere waterproofing alone, but only by a comprehensive water control program.

Keeping the Surface Water Away

The most common source of water is the sky. Since it is still popular to build underground homes on hills, and hills are great water catchers, they have a real affinity for funneling all that rain water right down on top of that lovely building site you've selected. Would you like to have a WHOLE MOUNTAIN of water pour over your home? Yet, that's exactly what some houses have; especially when the snow melts in the spring.

So, avoid this problem from the very beginning. When you pick out that beautiful spot, and you take all your relatives to where they are sure you've planned your "hermit's cave," don't take them there on some sunny Sunday afternoon. Take them there IN THE RAIN!

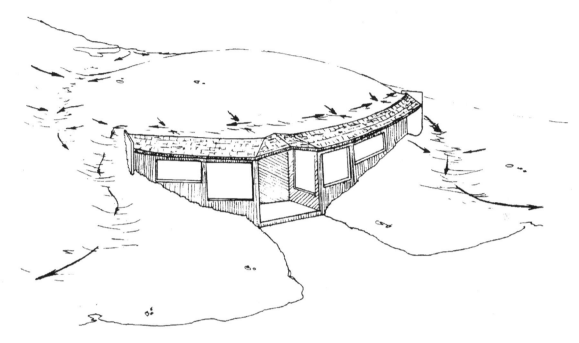

Figure 14 Sculpted land controls the surface water runoff.

Then, while they are laughing and pointing their fingers at the rushing torrent that's inundating your preciously picked place, TAKE NOTE! A little adjustment in the prospective position may preclude a big bill for "excavational earth reorganization." Don't plan so that you have to move a mountain. It's far easier to move the plan.

The land that is to be moved around should be sculptured to facilitate the easy runoff of rain water which falls on the roof, and to prevent water that gathers elsewhere from running onto the home, INCLUDING ITS HEAT STORAGE MASS. Always encourage the water to move AWAY from the home. This is done naturally by any good excavator. But other items he can't change such as the elevation of the house with respect to the land, the location and shape of driveways, entryways, window wells and the like can back up tons of water in some of the least desirable places, so these must be planned carefully.

But don't use the word "sculptured." Excavators charge more for "sculpturing" than for "sloping."

What if you're stuck with a big collecting bowl like a patio, etc., and you have to do something with all that water? Outdoor floor drains are very popular, and often quite sensible if installed properly. All too often, they are put at the bottom of a staircase, ramp, driveway or other outdoor water collector with the lowest part right smack against the house.

Have you ever seen such a drain that worked? Aren't they generally all clogged up with leaves, dead grass, old plastic sacks, and cigarette packages? If you are forced to use them, and use them only when you are FORCED TO; take positive steps to prevent them from being clogged up. A drain cap with large holes will help reduce clogging, but not with holes so large that they allow the pipe itself to clog. Make sure that the drain entrances are located in the spot where the water is actually going to be, especially after the concrete and the earth beneath it have settled. This collection place must be deep and wide enough so that the water doesn't back up under the door or even the insulation/watershed umbrella before it has time to drain away.

You should watch carefully what you hook these storm drains to. Sumps are popular but if they are in soil that doesn't drain well they probably aren't going to drain any better through a small sump. So you will probably have to make the drain-pit much bigger to give the water that is collected more time to soak into the soil. If you use a sump, make sure you can open it up to clean it. Silt can very easily clog a whole sump, even a big one!

Never connect a storm drain to a septic tank or a city sewer. A friend of mine had an indoor drain on the floor of his basement (about the same level where it probably would have been had it been an underground house). This floor drain was connected, along with the rest of his home's plumbing, to the city sewer system that also had storm drains connected to it rather than to the city storm-sewer system as they should have been. During spring run-off the sewer was very nearly full so it wouldn't take even the normal amount of waste water. So, through the floor drain, every time they did the laundry, the Tide® would come in.

How much better it would be if you could avoid catch basins altogether, or at least use a large storm drain even if it just goes around the house? If you do, you must keep all drainage sumps and pipes out of the heat storage zone, otherwise they will become unwanted earth tubes extracting heat just as if all this water were loose and flowing around.

Pondering Ponding Problems

Ponding problems occur whenever there is an accumulation of water in an unwanted place. The most familiar ponding problem shows up in the earth cover on top of a flat roofed underground home. Ponding has been a severe problem in some homes because most subterranean homes have flat roofs. Flat things are not very efficient at holding massive amounts of earth — especially heavy, wet earth. A large accumulation of water can actually cause a structural failure.

Water collects in the center of a flat roof. The roof, due to the increased weight, sags ever-so-slightly. The puddle gets bigger. The roof bends ever-so-slightly. The puddle becomes a pond. The roof flexes ever-so-slightly more. The pond becomes a lake. Then all of a sudden the lake goes away, to become an indoor pool!

You wouldn't build a perfectly flat above-ground roof, why build one below ground? If you do use a flat roof, set it at an angle so the water can run off of it, just as you would above ground. However curved roofs like domes, culverts, and other shell structures work much better, not only because they can be made stronger, and require a lot less materials, but because they shed the water rather than allow it to accumulate.

If however, you design for a small storage zone on the roof, as well as a moderation zone by including some earth between the insulation and the roof, potential ponding problems can be prevented by using the insulation/watershed umbrella because it encourages the water to drain safely away.

Roof ponding is not the most serious water control problem; mainly because so many fine texts have brought it to the fore. However, another sort of ponding has not been dealt with to such an extent. This is the kind of problem that is all too often designed into some homes, ponding that usually gathers less water, but occurs in sensitive, hard to deal with places.

Surface ponds or flowing streams of water can cause difficulties at those places where a portion of the home must protrude through the earth. The intersection of earth, flashing, waterproofing, and building can be hard enough to handle, without collecting water on the roof and then directing it right smack into these sensitive areas. Unfortunately, the earth tends to angle down toward these delicate places, because we like to have lots of earth cover that tapers off at the front of the roof. Retaining walls are especially famous for this. They can easily form a water control problem that can be handled easily by simply directing the run-off someplace else.

A good retaining wall has "weep" holes at its base so that water will not build up behind it, and as often happens; bring down even the biggest ones. Selective, controlled, run-off will reduce this amount to a trickle, and will prevent water from backing up along the retaining walls into the house. To accomplish this, we must keep the water flowing on top of the umbrella a little ways back from the top of the wall, and not right against it where the collected run-off could seep down between the umbrella and the wall. (Figures 14, 15, 22)

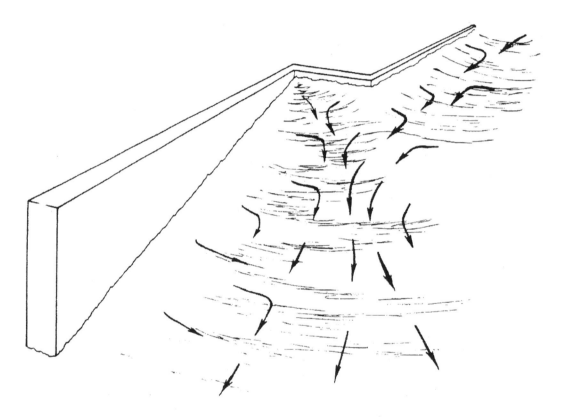

Figure 15 Backfill should be sloped so the water will not run right up against anything that must protrude from the earth cover, and especially those places where the insulation/watershed umbrella must come near or through the surface.

Surface water, collected into little streams on top of an earth shelter, can eat away the carefully placed earth cover to expose the insulation. This leaves a gaping crevasse at the corners of the roof and down behind retaining walls. Erosion is sneaky. It is slow but relentless. We can try to keep the velocity of the water to a reasonable level, but all such collection streams should be lined with a good stone or gravel base. Such stream beds will be a very functional part of the landscaping. But the best way to prevent erosion and control the surface water, in addition to proper sloping and direction is with green plants.

Green Roofs

Earth sheltered homes CAN be more beautiful than any above ground home. Do I say that just because of personal taste? No. The primary decoration of a properly designed underground home is green vegetation. Well laid out landscaping is composed of natural things: trees, bushes, grass, rocks, flowers, vines and shrubbery of all types. Drive down a quiet street, the most beautiful one in any town. What is it that makes it beautiful? Isn't it the huge trees hanging like decorated arches over the street, the well-manicured lawns, and the great variety of shrubs and flowers that make such a place so much more desirable to live in? Even in the older sections of town, where the homes are beginning to look a little shabby, isn't it the landscaping that has remained beautiful long after the luster of new construction has worn off? Who wouldn't want to have a park-like home in his neighborhood, one with the most beautiful of decorations as its major feature?

However ten hours behind a growling grass gobbler is not my idea of a "pleasant weekend at home!" There is no reason why all that newly found green space has to be laid out like a golf course, unless you golf a lot. Now, you certainly don't have to mow bushes, and the slightly longer growing season on the roof makes it a fine place for a vegetable garden. Remember though, to keep the moderation zone deep enough to save your insulation umbrella from your shovel! But even if you do have to use a lot of grass, remember, a well-designed earth shelter needn't have any maintenance that can't be done by a sheep!

Figure 16 Proper water control makes earth sheltered roofs green and eliminates the usual roof-top "deserts."

A marvelous variety of plant life is available from little tiny seeds, but before you select your favorites, you should take into consideration:
1.   The root system.
2.   The amount of water and sunlight that each needs.
3.   The climate and the new longer growing season on top of the storage zone.
4.   The weight.
5.   The usefulness for control of erosion, animals and people.
6.   The beauty of each.
7.   Their positions relative to each other, and the home.

Many conventional earth sheltered homes are deserts up on top, the "brown spot" on a green hill; because the roof with its thin waterproofing protection must be drained completely dry. The insulation/watershed umbrella will keep the home and the earth near it dry, but the moderation zone on top should be made with a high humus soil which will retain just the right amount of water for good plant growth. The earth cover on the roof should NOT be drained dry, but the umbrella's interior should.

Trees and some deep-rooted bushes should be avoided because the engineering may not allow for the extra weight, and we want to confine the roots to the two-foot-deep moderation zone. The plastic insulation umbrella will tend to localize roots in the moderation zone, while preventing them from growing into the umbrella, because it is dry both in and under it, and roots follow moisture.

So, you can landscape a subterranean home as if you were painting a picture. Just use your imagination and those natural tools: green plants.

Simultaneous Solutions with the Insulation/Watershed Umbrella

If you look out toward the Geodome (the working example of Chapter 1) you'll see that it is a green spot on a brown hill. The reason is that it has an insulation/watershed umbrella. Five moisture sensors were placed in the earth around this building. The top one in the upper earth-layer, the moderation zone, has been moist since the first rain storm after construction. The earth there is about two feet deep to allow room for good plant growth. Under the umbrella it is bone dry, or nearly so, all the way down to the footings.

The home's entire earth environment is dry in spite of the clay hill in which it is buried, where the water comes down in sheets during spring run-off. The proper level of moisture in the moderation zone can be controlled by placing the insulation/watershed umbrella between that which we want to be moist, (the top layer of earth called the moderation zone) and that which we want to be dry, (the storage zone, and the home in it). This plastic barrier will solve our dilemma by separating these two major water-related earth functions:

First: Keeping the EARTH around the home DRY makes waterproofing very easy, eliminates ponding, and prevents transportive heat flow from robbing our heat storage bin. Also, dry earth has a higher R-value which reduces heat loss out the end of the umbrella, while allowing the establishment of a permanent warm storage zone.

Second: The moist earth on top insures a well-functioning moderation zone, prevents erosion and fire, reduces the amount of watering needed, and keeps the roof beautifully green.

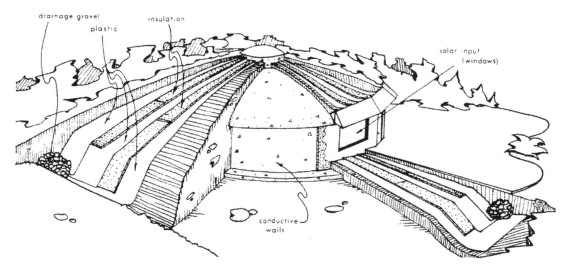

Figure 17 Cutaway view of the INSULATION/WATERSHED UMBRELLA. It is carefully put together with three layers of polyethylene plastic sheets, laid like shingles, with insulation between, and a layer of protective earth on top.

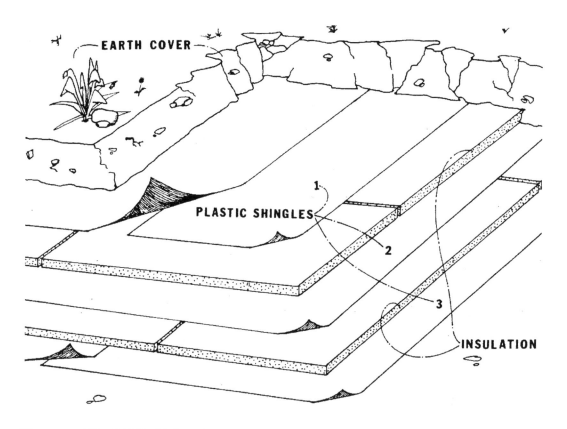

Figure 18 The INSULATION/WATERSHED UMBRELLA is made of at least three layers of plastic with two layers of insulation sandwiched between.

The INSULATION/WATERSHED UMBRELLA is the major component for proper underground water control. But why is it so different?

Underground Water Control

Pick up any text on underground houses, and you'll find the same pictures of subterranean walls with footing-level drain tile, loads of expensive waterproofing, and a river of water drenching the house. (I suspect they were first drawn by waterproofing salesmen.) Water flow problems persist.

Conflicting claims by the waterproofing industry haven't helped much in solving the water troubles, and rapidly rising waterproofing costs have made earth sheltering even more difficult, and costly. Just lately we've seen a number of pictures in magazine articles, that show a second drain tile near the TOP of the wall to reduce water flow, both for thermal and waterproofing reasons. That is a little better, but still far from ideal.

Look closely at Figure 19. Note that there is NO drain tile around the perimeter of the insulation/watershed umbrella, but there is a layer of gravel. Drain tiles remove water much faster than gravel, too fast for keeping the proper moisture content in most soils. By using gravel, the excess is drained away, while the moderation zone will retain just enough water to make those "deserts" blossom.

The SHAPE of the umbrella is also important. It is round, and like a fireman's hat, it's designed to make the water run off of it. Why else would it be called it an "umbrella?" Generally, people do not always equate the way things work above ground and the way they work below ground. But, despite the difference in position, materials, and installation sequence, the principles of operation are the same.

The water will run off the underground umbrella just like it does off the roof of an above-ground home.

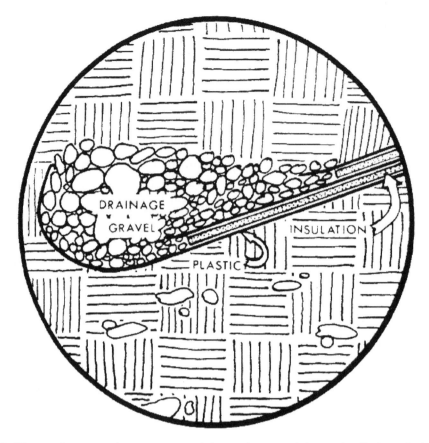

Figure 19 The underground gutter around the perimeter of the umbrella has drainage gravel inserted between plastic layers wherever there is no insulation to drain the entire umbrella.

Plastic Underground

The best construction material for use in underground water control is PLASTIC. No one I know, personally, would screw in a light bulb by turning the ladder! Every product has its preferred method of application, and its individual attributes. Yet people persist in installing plastic improperly and even showing it installed wrong in many how-to books. Then they belittle it for the problems that result (or they think result). While it is bad-mouthed by the waterproofing salesmen, they generally, when all is said and done, recommend that at least one layer of it be put over the top of their super-good product!

Polyethylene sheet plastic, often called "Visquine," is generally used in very large sheets, 20 x 100 feet (6 x 30 meters), and 0.006 inches thick (0.15 millimeters). This thickness is usually chosen because it is the thickest, and toughest of the garden variety plastic you can get for a very reasonable cost. It has some fine attributes:

1. It is the least expensive of any commercial water-control material.
2. It is not biodegradable and will last a long time.
3. It is fairly slippery.
4. Almost nothing will stick to it, even glue.
5. It is a complete water and vapor barrier.
6. It comes in very large segments.
7. Water will not only drain off the top of it, but will run under it too. (You probably think I put this one in the wrong list, but I didn't, as you will see.)

It also has some drawbacks that require the installer to be cautious.

1. It can be punctured easily.
2. It cannot be stretched and will hold no weight.

If it is installed properly it will do a fine job of underground water control. In order to use it properly we must remember the five things that can destroy it or render it useless:

1. **Sunlight.** The ultraviolet light from the sun will eventually turn it to powder. If stored out in the open for a long period of time it will deteriorate and not work as well when it is used. Now, the sun doesn't shine underground, so, only where the plastic has to protrude above the surface must it be protected with flashing.

2. **Burrowing animals.** If you live in an area where there are a lot of ground squirrels or gophers, don't put out a trap line. Remember, that they were smart enough to live underground long before you discovered subterranean living. But they don't have any plastic to control the underground water for their homes, so they like to dig where it's already dry. Ah ha! If you keep the roof of your home moist, as suggested, then they will move out to become your neighbors, rather than pests. If you plan your landscaping to match the arid climate that you already live in, and would like it to blend in with the scenery, protect the umbrella with lots of big rocks. The little fellows are tough, but usually not that tough. Now, it is true that muskrats and beavers burrow too, but if you have trouble with these, I'd suggest that you have a big enough water problem to warrant building elsewhere.

3. **Frost.** Frost will destroy it. When plastic gets cold, it gets brittle. When it moves it breaks. If it moves a lot, it breaks up in little pieces. Frost is accompanied by both low temperatures and movement. Of course, the purpose of the insulation in the "insulation umbrella" is to keep the earth beneath it at a higher temperature than the earth above it. With the storage mass at about 70° (21° C) some heat will pass through the insulation into the moderation zone. This accounts for the longer growing season. It also prevents freezing close to the umbrella. Also, the formation of frost requires the presence of water, and as we shall see, the entire umbrella will be so well drained that it will be dry. If you are in an area of extreme cold, like the Yukon, a small layer of round river gravel placed on top of the umbrella should keep that earth somewhat dryer. So a balance must be found between the requirements for drainage and for water retention based on the site's prerequisites.

4. **People who like to dig holes on their roofs.** So keep the dirt on top of the umbrella deep enough.

5. **People, by improper installation or by stomping it full of holes!**

To expect plastic to do a job that it was not designed to do is unwise, like the light bulb and the ladder. In all but a few of the examples I have seen, the plastic has been INSTALLED IMPROPERLY. So, proper installation is vital if we expect it to do the job for us.

Holes

The biggest complaint that people seem to have about plastic is that it gets holes in it. There really is no reason outside of just plain carelessness why it need be perforated. If the workmen are aware of its importance, and know how it should be installed, then it will survive construction to do the fine job it is capable of doing.

The plastic will soon be covered with dirt, dirt that could cause some holes to develop. Therefore, it would seem wise to avoid using a layer of crushed-stone gravel that has a lot of sharp pointed rocks in it, right on the plastic. The covering soil should only have round river stone, if any, since it will make fewer holes. However, holes – at least some holes – WILL be made.

Do you worry about holes? Let's consider some of the ways that plastic has been used in the past, and determine if there is an improved method of installation that will lessen this dastardly problem.

Some earth shelters have been waterproofed with just a single layer of plastic. Even today, thousands of homes have been built with All Weather Wood Foundations. They have been very successful. Their primary waterproofing system is gravity drainage, and a single layer of plastic.

Some earth shelters have been built with a multi-layer system, where six or eight layers of plastic are laid on top of each other for greater protection. But what happens when a rock or something punctures a hole in it? And it WILL HAPPEN. If you have one layer, how many holes are punched in the plastic? ONE. If you have 8 layers of plastic, and a rock batters an opening, how many holes will you now have? You guessed it: EIGHT HOLES! Eight CONCENTRIC holes! So, using multiple layers is probably not a whole lot better than a single one. Certainly, the top layer is the most effective.

Second problem: MULTIPLE HOLES. Over the entire surface of the insulation/watershed umbrella quite a number of holes may be made. Care will keep it to a minimum, but holes will be made. How much water will be funneled through these holes? Well, what is the total surface area of the first plastic sheet in comparison to the total surface area of all the holes put together? Obviously, the river of water that would ordinarily slosh over the home has been immediately REDUCED TO A TRICKLE!

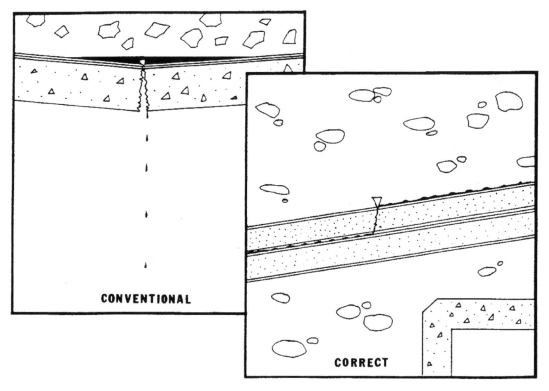

Figure 20 When a whole happens in an old fashioned waterproofing system, or in an INSULATION/WATERSHED UMBRELLA, a few trickles of water are far easier to cope with than an accumulated pond.

Plastic Protection

Plastic sheets should be laid like shingles, so the water which is missed by one shingle (goes through a hole,) is captured by a layer beneath it.

When a hole is made, especially by a stone, it usually doesn't penetrate very far. Therefore, a protective layer put between TWO layers of plastic will provide:

1. Protection for the second layer of plastic, so it will not be punctured.
2. A second layer which is also an UNDERGROUND SHINGLE, to catch the few trickles that make their way through the top shingle.

3. A means of drainage BETWEEN the layers so that the plastic can do its thing.

Often waterproofing salesmen are down on plastic because the water will travel beneath it for quite a long way. True, if it is just laid on the house as is usually done, with a torrent of water flowing over it and a leak occurs, it is just about impossible to find because where it goes in is usually a long way from where it comes out. Certainly it would be expensive to dig the whole thing up to find one hole.

So why does the water run just UNDER a sheet of plastic? For the same reason it always runs down your arms to drip off your elbows whenever you're trying to wash your face.

Should you then go out and buy some ooie-gooie-sticky stuff like tar or bentonite to put all under it to prevent the water from moving? No, this would only PREVENT the plastic from doing the dandy job it was designed to do. On the contrary! Provide a means of drainage under the plastic, between the separate layers used on the insulation/watershed umbrella. The top layer will encourage the water to travel just underneath itself, and the lower layer will catch any water that gets through, so those drops can trickle out of the way, just as they do on cedar shakes.

Conveniently, right between these two layers of plastic is the exact location where we want to put our insulation! Rigid insulation comes in convenient 4 x 8 feet or 2 x 8 feet (1.2 x 2.4 or 0.6 x 2.4 meters) boards that will encourage the water to runoff between, above, and below themselves until these few trickles reach a more desirable location. A very compatible marriage.

In most installations, it is generally recommended that about 4 inches (10-11 centimeters) of insulation be used in the insulation umbrella. Since these boards come in convenient thicknesses like 2 inches (5 centimeters) it would seem sensible to use THREE LAYERS OF PLASTIC with TWO LAYERS OF INSULATION sandwiched in between. This third layer of plastic would be the "back-up" layer, and would also be protected by the second layer of insulation which is above it. (Figure 18)

Each successive sheet of plastic will catch what trickles through from above, and each will drastically reduce any water flow eventually keeping the entire earth environment about the house D-R-Y!

Failure to use these fine attributes of plastic sheeting is like leaving your best tools out to rust or trying to drive nails with a rock!

Subterranean Shingles

Once upon a time, while building a house in Helena, Montana, I watched some hard working fellows roof a garage across the street from where we were building. They worked hard and soon had their back-breaking task complete. However, they had installed their seal-down shingles starting from the TOP of the gable! For those readers who have never roofed a house before, shingles work well, only if the water from each shingle is allowed to run off onto the TOP of the shingle beneath it, and so forth down the roof. In order for the shingles to be thus installed, one MUST begin at the EAVE, so that each succeeding shingle overlaps the one below it. Had it rained on this garage, the owner would have had a near-perfect indoor sprinkling system. The next week the guys were back, installing a second layer, starting from the eave.

Underground shingles, in the form of large plastic sheets, work basically the same. Even underground, water flows downhill. It never flows uphill unless you seal off its escape route so that it fills up the space between the plastic layers of the umbrella. Nevertheless, given proper drainage, large plastic shingles will move the water from where you get it, to where you want it. Just like their above-ground counterparts. Thus the plastic should be laid as if it were large shingles, with the upper shingle overlapping the lower adjacent one even though it is underground.

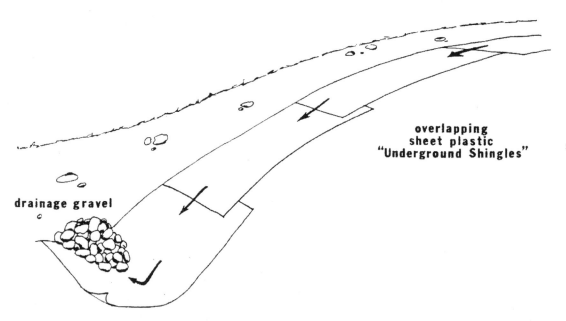

overlapping
sheet plastic
"Underground Shingles"

drainage gravel

Figure 21 Underground shingles, each one overlaps the one below it to direct underground water away from the home.

Unlike above-ground shingles, the underground shingle in the insulation/watershed umbrella must contend with some new problems. The earth over it will settle. This settling will be uneven. If you do not watch closely during installation, to see that a steep enough slope is provided, the earth may settle enough to back water up under the overlap of the adjacent up-hill shingle, or maybe even create a lake.

The earth will move some, so it is important to provide an arrangement that will ALLOW for it. Since plastic will not withstand ANY stretching. The overlaps (slip-joints) between adjacent plastic pieces must be fairly large (1 or 2 feet [30-60 cm]). Then as movement does occur, a gap will not suddenly appear between them. Please note carefully the illustration. (Figure 21)

Umbrella Drainage and Underground Gutters

Each of the three successive layers of plastic MUST HAVE DRAINAGE. (Figure 18) The insulation will provide drainage space in the main body of the umbrella. At the outer edges of the umbrella, the insulation should be tapered in one inch increments until there is just one inch left. (The thermal reasons for this are explained in Chapter 5 under: developing the thermal arrangement.) Therefore, at the outer edge of each insulation layer there MUST be a layer of round river stone, wherever there is no insulation between the plastic shingles, to allow drainage into a plastic gutter which is an extension of the bottom layer of plastic. (Figure 19) Otherwise, the earth will press the outer layers of plastic together, and the insulation will fill up with water. Each drainage layer should be terminated inside this perimeter gutter to catch all of the water that trickles its way out.

The water which runs off any roof should be caught in a gutter. So it is with the insulation/watershed umbrella; the first (top) and second layers of plastic, out at the edge of the umbrella, empty onto the third sheet. This bottom layer is extended out from under the umbrella in the shape of a GUTTER. Because that is exactly what it is—an underground gutter. It must be shaped like a gutter or ditch full of rocks, so that the water will not simply run over the edge.

If you live in a particularly wet area, you may wish to make this gutter fairly large, and use large stone, 3 inches (8 centimeters) or more, to encourage faster removal. If you live in a VERY WET climate, the plastic gutter should be extended quite a distance past the end of the insulation to keep the water as far away from the home as possible. Even a drain-tile could be included; after all, if it gets to dry on top you could always stop the tile up a little bit at the end to slow down the drainage.

This gutter must contain the water and it MUST RUN DOWNHILL along the perimeter of the umbrella. It should start at a high point in the center, unless there is a reason why you don't want the water to run out both sides. Angle it just like drain tile, one quarter inch to the foot (2 centimeters to the meter), and bring the end to "daylight." It may be more convenient to "daylight" a short stub of tile, but it would be cheaper and look far nicer to bring the gravel to daylight using big rocks. (Figure 24)

Often a single layer of newspaper or straw is put on top of underground drainage gravel before the top soil goes on. Its purpose is to prevent the fine soil from sifting down to clog the gravel, until the soil can become packed tight enough to prevent it naturally.

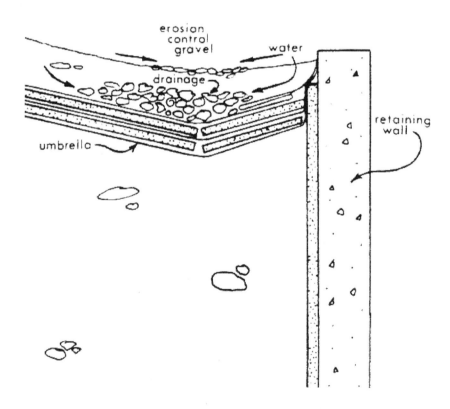

Figure 22 Surface and below ground water should be gathered into gutters well away from delicate spots like retaining and parapet walls.

The outer edges of the umbrella should be installed carefully, especially where they meet retaining walls, parapet walls and other protrusions of the structure through the earth cover because they are gathering points for a LOT OF WATER, and the last thing you want to do is funnel it UNDER the umbrella, behind the walls or cause it to run down over the front of the house. Here too, a similar underground gutter should be used, along with the surface contouring, so the accumulated water can be kept back away from the building. These are the difficult areas that must be designed with great care, and installed with even greater care. (Figure 22)

Now the home and its storage mass should be DRY.

The Vapor Barrier

The last layer of plastic that any moisture may encounter, and the first layer to actually be installed, is the vapor barrier. Keeping the running water many feet away from the actual structure will certainly make waterproofing much simpler, and far cheaper. However, moisture, usually non-moving moisture, will still exist in most soils. Therefore, a vapor barrier is vital. This is the layer that is draped over the house itself.

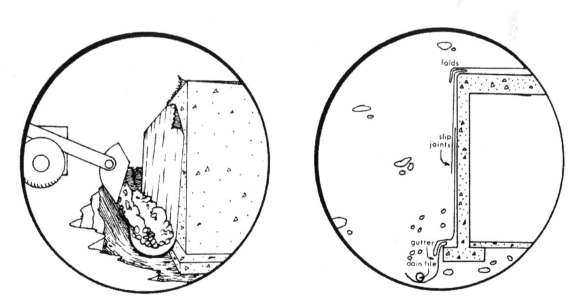

Figure 23 Plastic should never be draped over the building. The right method of installing plastic over a building allows the plastic to settle down with the backfill by using folds and overlapping slip-joins laid like shingles.

Installing the vapor barrier is a little more difficult than the umbrella. We must not actually "drape" it over the structure and then backfill. The heavy backfill will pull the plastic down, stretch it, and if not right away then later when the dirt settles, it will TEAR OFF like a paper towel from a rest room towel dispenser.

Form a gutter at the bottom of the footing; under the drain tile if you choose to use one. At the footing, the top of the walls, and whenever the shape takes a major change in direction, an OVERLAPPING FOLD should be included along with a 1- or 2-foot (30- or 60-centimeter) wide slip-joint (shingle overlap) wherever a new piece of plastic must be added. As you work your way up the wall, these folds and overlaps should be arranged so that they will be able to slip or UN-fold as the dirt settles, thus at no time will there be any tension on the plastic. But don't fold it like a catch basin. Fold it so that it will always allow the water to run off of it. (Figure 23) And keep it away from sharp edges. In fact, try to avoid building any sharp edges in the first place.

Unroll the plastic as backfilling is taking place. Don't try to hold up the earth with it. It won't work! Allow it to settle down with the earth as backfilling is in progress, while being careful to allow enough folds and overlaps to remain for future earth settling.

Now that we've taken care of the surface water, the running underground water, the vapor and the moisture in the soil, you next must deal with the moisture which can be sponged up by the concrete itself and the water table.

A Concrete Sponge

Can you imagine a concrete sponge? Concrete is a fairly effective water barrier for the most part. It has only two drawbacks. First: It will soak up water from the bottom of the footings by capillary action, allowing it to evaporate into the dwelling, and Second: It cracks. There are several ways of preventing the capillary action. The first is very effective, but not generally known. Almost all concrete is made in what is called a "5 ½ sack mix." That means that for every cubic yard of concrete that is made, there are five and one half 94 pound (42.6 kilogram) sacks of Portland cement in it. If the amount of cement per yard is increased to seven sacks its waterproofing ability is increased several MILLION times, especially if you use as little water as possible when mixing it. A less expensive method is to use a concrete additive that will make it waterproof.

There are a number of fine products on the market called "integral waterproofers." After considering a number of these, we settled on a particular one called Berylex. It is fairly inexpensive; it makes concrete waterproof; it makes it stronger; it bonds old concrete to new concrete like you wouldn't believe and it coats the steel with chromium to help preserve it. It is available from Berylex National Sales, Kansas City, MO. You just pour it into the cement truck before you pour out the mud, and it does the trick. (By the way, they didn't pay me to say that. It did for me exactly what they said it would and you sure can't say that for a lot of other people's stuff I've bought!)

However, cracks can still occur, and it is these cracks for which so many of the waterproofing people have tried to design their products. The Berylex will help reduce some types of cracking. However, bad cementing practice has more to do with cracking than any other problem. Making good concrete is a little like baking a cake: a little change in the recipe can make a big change in the taste, and if you jump on the floor at the wrong time, the whole thing can fall. So, know your concrete!

Some other methods of crack control include good engineering and the use of pre-stressing and post tensioning techniques. Without these special tensioning methods, concrete MUST crack.

YIKES A CRACK! Why on earth MUST it crack? Because the steel in it will not begin doing its job by going into tension until the concrete cracks. These cracks are just hairline cracks. If they spread to an eighth inch (3 millimeter) or so wide you've got real engineering headaches. The whole problem with cracks is that water will run through them. If the entire body of earth around the home is dry because of the insulation/watershed umbrella so what if the concrete does crack? No water, no leak!

However, in critical areas, like where the home protrudes through the earth, it is far more difficult to keep these areas away from the water. Here special water proofing agents may be prudent.

Hydrostatic Pressure

If you dig a hole for your dream home and you hit an Artesian well, I suggest you make beer, and move the house someplace else! Just because the umbrella wipes out the problems of water which comes in from above is no reason to ignore the water which comes up from below. When you are investigating a building site, one of the priority prerequisites should be that the water table is sufficiently low to permit construction. Check it out, and not in the dry season either when the water table is low.

Earth sheltered homes are NOT made to withstand hydrostatic pressure. Actual hydrostatic pressure occurs when the home is submerged in water. NEVER should such a condition be allowed to exist. The tremendous force of actual hydrostatic pressure will buckle a concrete floor, crack a wall, or at the very least, bring springs of the water deep into your living room.

Some waterproofing salesmen will boast that their product will withstand such gigantic amounts of pressure that it could float your home in the ocean. Are you designing an underground submarine? Why waterproof for something which (structurally) must never be allowed to occur anyway? Gravity drainage is the ONLY proven way to prevent hydrostatic pressure. Water that isn't there can't cause problems.

Backfill Drainage

Unless there is some way to actually find out, you don't have the foggiest notion what's going on behind the walls of an underground home. However, the drainage system will tell, if it has its drain-exit outdoors. If a well-designed sump must be used, it should be one that can be examined easily to see if any water is or has been present. By watching it, one will be able to find out if any water is getting back there at all. Since no one wants to stay up all night and watch a pipe, a small piece of cloth may be laid a foot or so up into the pipe; one that that won't clog it. If any water does run over the cloth, it will remain moist for quite a while so it can be checked at leisure. Most importantly, if you bring the drainage system to "daylight," out in the open so you can see it, you will completely drain the back fill.

A popular drainage system is the so-called French drain. French drains are simply a gravel-filled trench a foot or so from the building, and as deep as the wall. They will do the job in all but the worst of circumstances. But in most cases a full gravel backfill works better and is easier to install. If the soil on the job site drains fairly well, it can be used instead of straight gravel. The backfill can be "daylighted" with a ditch full of big rocks at the opening, or a short piece of pipe can go from the bottom of the backfill gravel to daylight. At the bottom of the wall where the water collects, it is a good idea to make a small gutter out of plastic so it can catch any running water that may get under the umbrella and channel it to daylight. Otherwise it would probably just drain into the earth and not speak to you about what's going on back there. (Figures 23 & 24)

If the soil you build in has high clay content, it will exert an abnormally high lateral (sideways) pressure on the walls. Gravel on the other hand will reduce this pressure to where it will have a pressure of about 20 pounds per square foot per foot of depth (320 kilogram per square meter per meter of depth), whereas even regular soil will press at about 30 pounds per square foot (480 kilogram per square meter per meter of depth), and much more in clay. Gravel will exhibit little or no settling, does not require a special trench, and it's cheap. If you do not have a fast draining soil already, a round river gravel backfill is the best idea.

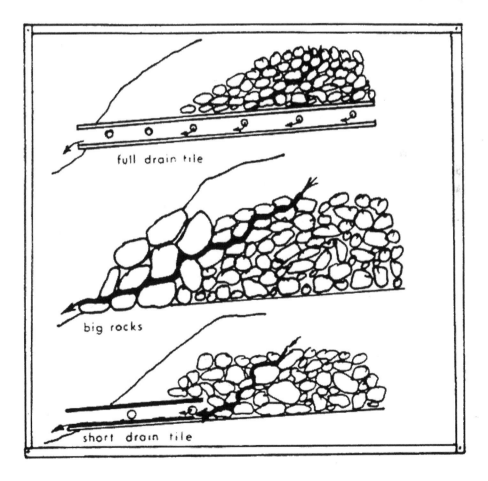

Figure 24 Three ways to bring the lowest portion of the backfill drainage system, or the outer rim of the umbrella, to "daylight."

Drain Tile and the Shape of the Backfill Hole

Drain tile (usually 4 inches (10 centimeters) of plastic pipe with holes in it) is often used with gravel. It drains faster, but may only be needed in wet climates. It seems to be easier to explain this arrangement using tile than just gravel on top of the plastic gutter. Let's talk about how to install the tile while remembering that it works the same with drain tile as without. If you choose to use tile or not the plastic gutter must be laid out just the same. That is, the bottom of the backfill hole must be shaped like a gutter, and the gravel (with or without tile) is put on top.

Just about every text I've seen which describes how to keep underground walls dry, shows the drain tile being placed at the footing level, the bottom of the hole you've dug to put the house in. If someone were to install your sewer line, and lay it out with a transit to make it lay PERFECTLY LEVEL, how long would it be, before you threw a fit because it was all clogged up? Sewer or drain pipe is laid with about a quarter inch to the foot drop so the fluid will run downhill. When the footings were laid out, wasn't considerable time and effort used to lay the footings PERFECTLY FLAT? Then why on earth would anyone want the drain tile to lay beside the footers; perfectly level? The place where the tile lays must be sloped. The same holds true for the bottom of a gravel backfill unless the ground is all gravel anyway. The pipe's elevation with respect to the house determines how well it will work.

Lowering the Water Table

Let's consider the draw-down lines in Figure 25. These are lines that are supposed to show how the water table is altered by the insertion of a drainage system. The water table (the dotted lines) represent is the level of underground water. It is the water table that determines whether the earth around a subterranean home will be continually wet or dry.

Above the draw-down lines the earth is relatively dry, and below them it is wet. In gravel these lines are flat, because the water flow is so fast that it is like a bucket with a hole in its side. The level of water in the bucket will not rise above the hole. In clay soil the lines curve down to the pipe, since the flow to the side is not as quick as with gravel.

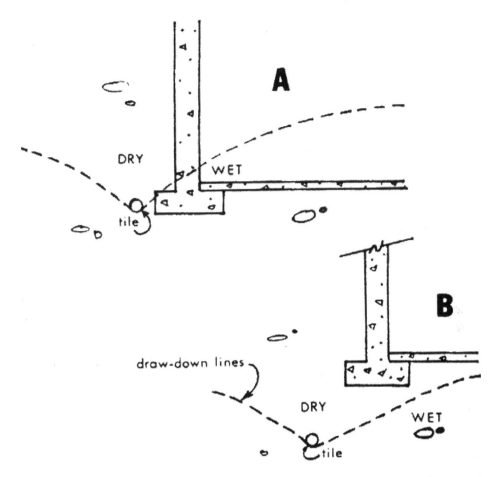

Figure 25 Draw-down lines are affected by the depth of the drain tile, and/or gravel drain. On the first one the floor is WET. On the second one the floor is DRY.

In soil which is not gravel-ish, and a draw-down curve exists, AND the pipe is located next to and level with the footing, (Figure 25-A) is the floor wet or dry? Since the curve goes upward from the tile, the floor is wet. Do you want a wet floor? When the drain system goes all the way around the house and the water has a way to drain under the footings, it is a lot harder for water to get under the floor. Slopping the tile a little (and/or putting gravel under the floor if the home is to be built in clay) levels out this line and keeps the floor dry (Figure 25-B)

The drainage system, whether just gravel, or gravel and tile, must also slope downhill from its highest point in the back of the house all the way around the home to daylight. That beginning HIGH POINT MUST BE AT LEAST A FOOT BELOW THE FOOTINGS, unless the home it being built in a gravel soil, and even then, it should NEVER START HIGHER THAN THE FOOTING. Otherwise you will have a WET FLOOR.

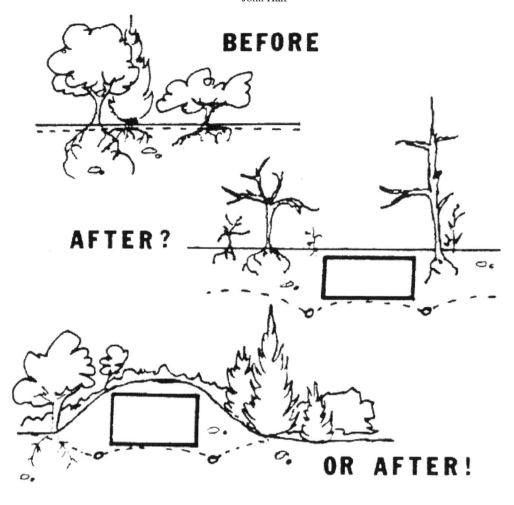

Figure 26 The water table is affected by the introduction of an artificial drainage system such as the one around an earth sheltered home. If the aquifer is high then the home should be raised up and bermed.

There is another factor which is all too often ignored in the site selection for an underground home. Insertion of the drainage system into the earth may significantly alter the natural water table. You have paid a lot of money for a nice green, plant covered site then you insert a drainage system which lowers the natural water table, the aquifer, and what do you get? Dead trees. The drainage system is vital for keeping the home dry, but it should be designed to keep it moist where you want it moist as well as dry where you want it dry. So raise the house up and berm it if you must, but don't significantly lower the natural water table.

A Clay Cap

A few people will be afraid of using just plastic, thinking that it will not last as long as they would like it to. Yet, there is no reason to believe that the plastic, which is NOT BIODEGRADABLE, will be any less permanent than clay. If one feels that way, then a couple of inches of clay could be put right over the top of the umbrella. It doesn't have to be pure bentonite (the stuff in clay that makes it stop water,) nor should it be bought by the bucket full. Buckets cost too much. It should be gotten as close to the building site as possible.

But what about waterproofing?

Waterproofing

I have just described a complete water control system designed to take care of every water source, except the kitchen sink! These methods not only work better but are less expensive than the conventional way of running a river of water over the home and then waterproofing the house as if it were a battleship! This ENTIRE program of water control IS the waterproofing! You must use ALL of it. For what reason would you need any more?

After all that, some of you will still want to put regular waterproofing on the house. As you wish, but be aware of what it actually does and then use it only where it is really needed. Otherwise, you may be just wasting a lot of money and still not getting the job done.

A complete program of water control IN the earth environment is essential; not only for keeping you dry, but for keeping you warm too.

Notes:

Chapter 5 – The Insulation Water/Shed Umbrella

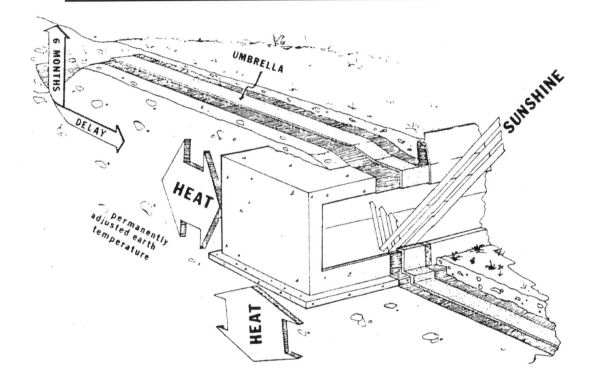

Developing the Heat Storage Arrangement

Many conventional earth shelters have trimmed regular space heating needs by 70 to 90 percent. Typically, it costs more each month to heat the domestic hot water than it does to heat the entire underground house. Yet, even in 1981 improvement seemed within easy grasp. The method of achieving the ultimate in energy conservation, Passive Annual Heat Storage, was evident from an examination of the shape, size, and configuration of the underground insulation then in use on many earth shelters.

This study resulted in the design of the insulation/watershed umbrella. One reason the insulation/watershed umbrella is shaped as it is, is because it sheds water, but how could a simple adjustment in the way insulation is used underground make such a big thermal difference. We can best understand how it works by following the thermal development of the umbrella.

The University of Minnesota reported using a sophisticated dynamic heat flow computer program to examine a number of insulation configurations. Their basic approach was: anybody can reduce the heat flow from a building by adding more insulation, but can the ARRANGEMENT of the insulation have a great effect on the operation of the building in this new, somewhat bewildering earth environment?

A standard insulation arrangement was chosen that had 4 inches (10 centimeters) of insulation on a roof earth sheltered with about 18 inches (46 centimeters) of dirt, and 2 inches (5 centimeters) of insulation on its subterranean walls. Using this standard configuration, the amount of insulation on the walls was then rearranged to determine if the home would work better. (Figure 27)

The first rearranged configuration (Figure 28) to be compared with the standard had the lower half of the wall's insulation removed and put on top of the upper half. The result was: 4 inches (10 centimeters) of insulation over the upper half of the wall, with the lower portion bare to the earth. A number of underground homes have been build using this kind of an insulation arrangement and have been quite successful, but just how good would it be?

The home's summertime performance (its ability to cool itself) increased by 10 percent. It would do a better job of keeping itself cool than would a house that used the standard insulation arrangement. But the wintertime performance decreased by 5 percent. This seems to be an overall improvement for places where cooling is more important than heating. However, the 5.6 foot reduction in the size of the isolation zone is a significant factor that makes the comparison more difficult to analyze.

What could account for this change? In Chapter 1, the basics of underground heat flow were laid out: The temperature in the ground is a reflection of the average annual air temperature at the nearest conductive surface. The amount of temperature fluctuation during the year depends upon the amount of temperature fluctuation at the surface, and the length of the conductive path.

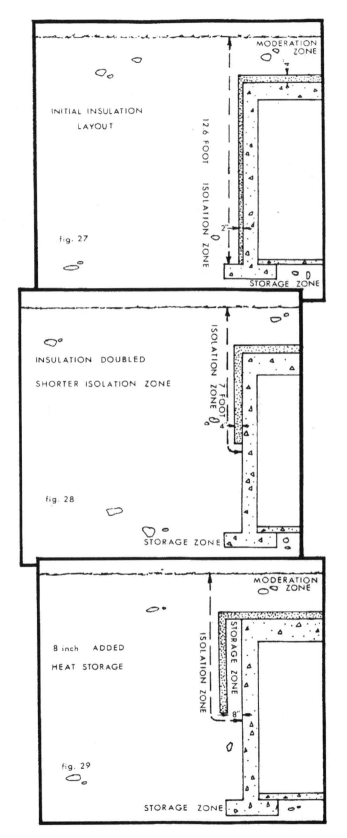

Figures 27 - 29
University of Minnesota computer analysis of different insulation arrangements.

There is no insulation separating the earth behind the home and the outdoor surface. (That is, there is no umbrella.) Therefore, the greater body of earth around the home has its temperature set more by the outdoor air temperature than the indoor temperature. Therefore, in cold climates the body of earth within 20 feet (6 meters) of the house will be cold. The heat from within the home will raise this temperature slightly. However, the surface area of the home is quite small in comparison to the surface area of the outdoor surface, and will therefore in this case, exert a much smaller influence than the outdoor temperatures.

The lower half of the wall is further from the conductive surface, than the upper half of the wall. Therefore, the isolation is greater than at the top of the wall. This difference has been made up in Figure 28 by the addition of insulation on the upper portion of the wall. However, the Isolation Zone is still much too small, because a 6-month time delay conductive path has not been provided. The results are as expected. The body of earth around the home is cool because of the insulation configuration. Therefore as we would expect, it would be easier to take heat out of the house, as in the summer time, and harder to heat the house in the wintertime. The structure continually loses heat. It just loses it slower than an above ground home.

The second case (Figure 29) provided an additional eight inches of insulation at the roof level (8 inches (20 centimeters) out from the wall, not in thickness,) so that the warm thermal mass of the upper wall could be increased by using some earth in addition to the concrete. The performance was astounding! The summertime ability to keep cool increased by 20 percent over the original standard configuration. The wintertime performance INCREASED by 0.09 percent over the standard configuration.

More importantly, the addition of only 8 inches (20 centimeters) of heat-storing earth next to the upper wall made the summertime operation about 10% and the wintertime operation about 5 percent better than Figure 28, which has the same foreshortened 7 feet (2 meters) of Isolation Zone. Outstanding for just adding eight tiny inches of dirt!

Is that what we should expect? Certainly, the upper portion of the wall represents one-half of the conductive surface of the structure on that one side. Although the 16 inches (40 centimeters) of isolated thermal mass (dirt and concrete together) produced thermal Storage Zone with only a day or so of storage ability, the results were remarkable enough to indicate that putting any insulation on the walls at all was counterproductive. However, the Isolation Zone was still so small that the greater body of earth around the home remains subject to outdoor surface temperature changes. Therefore the isolated Storage Zone is still quite small.

The third case (Figure 30) extended the insulation like a wing to the side of the home. (Remember, this is a computer study. In the real world, it's very difficult to prevent such a configuration from being sheared off by the dirt as the backfill settles.) The thermal idea was to increase the warm storage mass adjacent to the wall, isolating it from the outdoor temperature changes by increasing the heat flow paths through the earth. The summer performance increased a whopping 33.3% over the original arrangement, while the wintertime warming ability decreased by ONLY 2.5 percent. But, in comparison to figure 28 with its small, 7 feet (2 meters), of Isolation Zone, this wing-type arrangement is 23.3 percent better in the summer and 2.5 percent BETTER in the wintertime.

In comparison to Figure 29, with its extra 8 inches (20 centimeters) of earth, the wing-type arrangement came out on top in the summer by 13.3 percent. However, the 8 inches (20 centimeters) of dirt added to the top of the wall in Figure 29 was isolated by a 7-foot (2 meters) long heat conducting path through the earth, whereas the wing-type of figure 30 had only 22 inches (56 centimeters) at the far end of the insulation. Raising the insulation up allows the heat to flow around it so that thermally, the top of the wall is just within 7 feet (2 meters) of the surface negating much of what was added in Figure 29.

Obviously we can learn several things from this computerized comparison.

1. The 8-inch (20-centimeter) layer of earth in Figure 29 would rise to a higher temperature than the earth just under a wing because of having better isolation, therefore, the isolated 8 inches (20 centimeters) of dirt has become a Storage Zone. In the original arrangement only the concrete operated at room temperature, and constituted the only Storage Zone in a conventional earth shelter.

2. Since an Isolation Zone is just as capable of thermally separating a body of earth as it is a home, an effective isolation zone can be used to separate a Heat Storage Zone that can be maintained at just about any temperature we would like. Thus, a good Isolation Zone eliminates any need for wrapping insulation all the way around a subterranean home and its thermal storage mass.

3. Since Figures 27 & 29 had about the same wintertime performance, 7 feet (2 meters) of Isolation Zone must be a bare

minimum, and in very cold climates it would simply be TOO SHORT. The theoretical distance would provide 20 feet (6 meters) for the Isolation Zone, and another 20 feet (6 meters) for the Storage Zone, (6 months delay for each zone). However, because the actual temperature differences between the indoor average temperature and the outdoor average temperature are reasonably close to each other a compromise is clearly more practical, and cost effective. For most installations between the Arctic and Antarctic circles. 10 to 12 feet (3 to 4 meters) of Isolation Zone, and the same for a good Storage Zone, would seem to be much more practical. Since there is no clearly defined line between a Storage Zone and an Isolation Zone, it is only possible to define an approximate distance.

4. The extensive summer cooling which occurred in Figure 30 shows us that the isolated warm storage mass must be increased to a size large enough to accept, keep, and then return the much larger summertime heat flow from the house. Obviously more heat is being lost in the winter than is gained in the summer. If we can confine annual heat loss and gain to the exposed surface of earth sheltered home itself, then this annual balance of heat flow, becomes controllable, and we may adjust it as we wish.

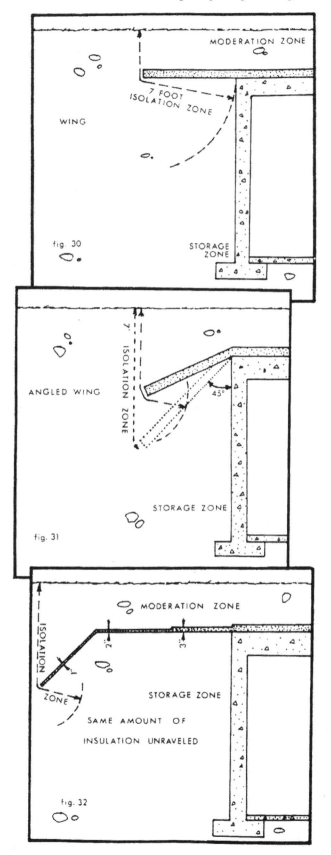

fig. 30

Figure 30 Wing-type insulation of the University of Minnesota study.

fig. 31

fig. 32

Figures 31 - 32 Optimizing the thermal arrangement using principles learned from the University of Minnesota study.

Optimizing

Some insulation wings like the ones described have been used since the Underground Space Center first suggested them, but why haven't they achieved full Passive Annual Heat Storage? There are two principle reasons why this arrangement still leaves the regular earth shelter with its surrounding earth controlled by the outdoor temperatures. First: They don't shed water to keep the stored heat from being washed away. Second: THEY HAVE ALL BEEN TOO SMALL. The 7 to 10 feet (2 to 3 meters) of conductive path is barely long enough to function as an Isolation Zone. Until now, it was assumed that only the house was in need of isolation. A much larger umbrella would provide thermal isolation not just for the house but for the warm Heat Storage Zone also. The earth next to the building under the small umbrella of Figure 30 could never be heated to room temperature because its temperature is still dominated by the large outdoor temperature swings.

Did the University of Minnesota have annual heat storage as a goal? No, they were pioneering a new technology themselves. Their work had to be accomplished first, before any practical method of year-long storage could be devised. Their goal was, first of all, basic energy efficiency. The primary aim of their computer analyses was to establish basic operating principles, and specifically, to show how the insulation may be rearranged to make the earth shelter work better without increasing the cost. We now have the opportunity to 'stand on the shoulders of these giants' and tackle the next task: optimizing the insulation arrangement. Having established the basic operating principles, we can choose an achievable goal: Passive Annual Heat Storage.

In the third computer trial (the wing in Figure 30) the winter performances were down a little in comparison to Figure 29 with its extra 8 inches (20 centimeters) of dirt. Therefore, more heat would be lost over the year rather than stored. The Isolation Zone was too small to allow for a Storage Zone even 8 inches (20 centimeters) thick. Since the goal is to increase storage mass by this arrangement, let's apply what we have learned, and try some other arrangements.

What if the insulation wing came down from the roof at a 45 degree angle (Figure 31, dotted lines,) and extended down to the seven foot level. The conductive path from the surface to the end of the insulation provides quite a bit of isolation due to its accumulated moderation and resistance, so that most of a year's changes have been averaged out; an effective Isolation Zone. This Isolation Zone is now located, not right against the building, but out on the end of the umbrella. The 45 degree angle would provide more storage mass next to the upper wall than just the eight inches of Figure 29 by extending the length of the Isolation Zone and insulating a larger earth mass. But wouldn't the straight wing example (Figure 30) provide even more?

NO! Remember that conductive heat flow doesn't care about gravity. It simply goes around the thermal obstacle taking the path of least resistance. The wing, only being a little over five feet long (150 centimeters) and about two feet (60 centimeters) from the surface, would barely allow even seven feet (213 centimeters) of isolating heat flow path before it would reach the upper wall. The fact that it did not work as well indicates that the isolation path must be made longer.

The 45 degree angle arrangement increases the Isolation Zone and the storage mass to boot. If the angle of inclination is set to somewhere between the flat wing and the 45 degree (Figure 31, solid lines) then the 7-foot (2-meter) Isolation Zone will extend a little further under the umbrella, but the storage mass is still about the same size as the 45 degree one. So the important principle is that it should angle down, but the exact angle is not critical.

In actual operation, we may encounter a wide variety of underground obstacles. It may not always be convenient to dip the umbrella's end at "just the right angle." In many cases, a slower, more even curve may nearly fit the natural slope made by earth-moving equipment even more. This shape is usually gentler if one uses a backhoe, rather than a front-end loader. Naturally it depends on the skill of the operator and the amount of time and money that is being put into the project, along with the terrain, and the soil make-up. The least expensive way is usually the one chosen. You need to know what can be done with the umbrella so its operation will not be impaired because of a big rock, lot line, or whatever happens to be in the way.

If the outer edge of the umbrella must be less than 4 or 5 feet (1.2 or 1.5 meters) from the final earth's surface, (flatter rather than curved down) it should be extended further out until the conduction path is about the same as the angled down arrangement would have been. If the obstacle is more vertical, like a retaining wall, then insulate the back of the retaining wall and then curve the insulation under at the bottom of the wall. (Figure 34) Remember that the conductive path goes to the nearest exposed surface by the path of least resistance regardless of gravity.

If a tree is encountered, you shouldn't just put a hole in the umbrella or try to run the umbrella closely around the tree. It will die of thirst!

You'll have to stop the umbrella before it gets to the tree. Here you could bring the umbrella straight down 7- to 10-feet (2-3 meters) in a trench several feet away from it to avoid either shortening the Isolation Zone, or cutting off the roots. If you wish to save certain trees, this is an important point to take into consideration when positioning the house, since the umbrella is just as much a part of the plan of the house as the retaining walls or the kitchen sink.

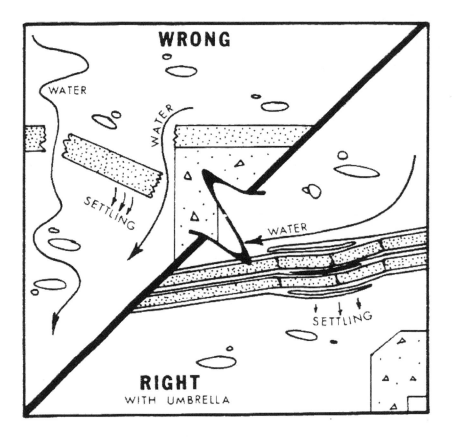

Figure 33 Extending the isolation and storage zones with a curved-under umbrella on the back of a retaining wall.

Now that we have determined the correct shape for the umbrella, let's look at what is happening out on the VERY END of the insulation.

Out on the End

The thickness of the insulation (Figure 31) is constant, but the temperature difference is not. For ease in thinking, consider the situation late in the winter. The home is warm. The Moderation Zone on the other side of the insulation up close to the house and on the roof is cold. Here, 4 inches (10 centimeters) of insulation seems to be adequate in most climates. But, what is the temperature differential, the difference between the temperature on one side of the insulation and the temperature on the other side, out ON THE END of the insulation? What is the path of least resistance? Isn't it through the dirt, around the end of the insulation? How much resistance is accumulated from a point on one side of the insulation to a point just opposite it? Small, in comparison to 4 inches (10 centimeters) of insulation! Then why pay all that money to put four inches of insulation out there when a much thinner amount will do?

The first inch (2.5 centimeters) of insulation has between 40 and 80 times the resistance as that same inch of dirt would be if the insulation were not there. Thus some insulation must be there or else no isolation will take place at all. Remember how well 2 inches (5 centimeters) of insulation worked in Figure 27, in comparison to Figure 28? However, the second inch is not as vital as the first one, while the cost is doubled. Therefore, the umbrella should be tapered, to match the change in temperature difference, down to a single inch at the outer edge, Start with about 4 inches (10 centimeters) near the building and then reduce it by an inch at fairly even intervals. (Figure 35)

The next step: If we unravel that SAME AMOUNT of insulation, extend it as far as we can, reducing its thickness, and bending the end down, (Figure 32) what a tremendous amount of storage mass is suddenly added, and without buying a single nickel's worth of extra insulation.

The last two computer test cases (Figures 29 and 30) were obviously superior to the original, commonly built, arrangement. So how come you don't see tons of earth shelters with either of these arrangements?

There are a few, but one factor seems to be holding them up. The settling of the backfill would destroy the insulation wing, causing "thermal short circuits." A thermal short circuit occurs whenever a large hole in the insulation allows heat to escape eliminating any benefit gained from the insulation; it's like having an open garage door in your dining room. So the ideal insulation layout must be able to deal with these subterranean changes.

Thermal Short Circuits & Settling Problems

What if the insulation were to be broken up by the settling backfill? (Figure 33) Destruction of the insulation can certainly occur next to a sharp-edged wall where everything will be scraped off the wall by the force of the settling earth, waterproofing, insulation, everything. And what about the built-in cracks between the 4 foot by 8 foot boards of the insulation itself? Will they not make thermal short circuits?

Heat will flow through these cracks. But, HOW will the heat get through them? By conduction? Conductive heat flow through the insulation umbrella, wing or whatever, is proportional to the square area of crack. [$Q=A\,(1/R)(T_2-T_1)$] What is the total surface area of all the cracks in comparison to the area of the insulation as a whole? Isn't it quite small? As long as the insulation is generally intact, NO appreciable amount of heat will flow through by conduction because the area is small.

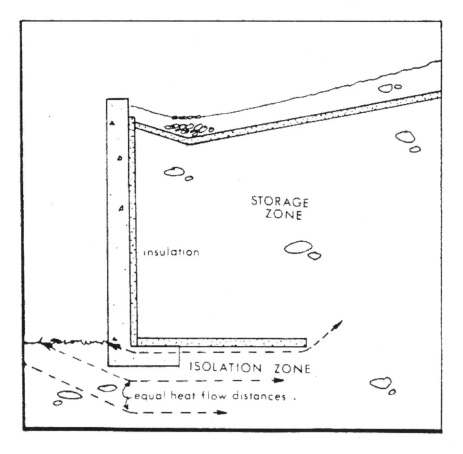

Figure 34 Thermal "Short Circuits" caused by the settling of the backfill, will be prevented by using an insulation/watershed umbrella.

However, heat can flow through these cracks, and it can become significant. It just doesn't do it by conduction. How then, does it get through? Certainly not by radiation! Remember transportive heat flow? Ah, of course! Water pours right through cracks. But what if the umbrella is made by sandwiching the insulation between three layers of plastic, as described in Chapter 4, raised up off of the sharp-edged wall, being designed so that insulation and backfill can settle together without tearing things up? VOILA! Water is stopped, heat flow stops, problem solved.

An Idealized Arrangement

Now we are able to inexpensively isolate a very large volume of heat-storing earth that can be passively heated to room temperature. The maximum distance through which we can, for all practical purposes, store and retrieve heat is about 20 feet (6 meters). An idealized arrangement would have to extend even further, to about 20 feet (6 meters) beyond the walls. But how far? Must it extend out so far that the arrangement becomes impractical? How big should the isolation zone be? Is seven feet enough?

Why was seven feet chosen in the first place? Experience with the homes that had been built up until 1979, made this a reasonable guess given the energy conservation goals of the day. But a guess never-the-less, and remember that there weren't nearly as many then as now. The 7-foot (6-meter) isolation zone was used in the computer examination of Figure 28 because of the basic restriction that was put on the whole analysis: the insulation should not cost any more than the original arrangement.

The insulation from the original configuration was doubled in Figure 28 and then laid out as a wing in Figure 30. So the actual amount of insulation in use was chosen, not for thermal reasons, but because of the normal height of an underground wall. A normal wall's height allows room for both structure and people. The amount of structure depends on the building's overall size, which is actually determined by the size of the people to be in them. Therefore the actual amount of insulation was chosen because of the typical height of a human being!

Logically, the size of the insulation, and thus the size of the Isolation, Storage, and Moderation Zones, should be selected for thermal reasons. The insulation arrangement in Figure 27 worked just about the same as Figure 29. The effect of cold winter weather takes two months to reach 7

85

feet 8 inches (2.34 meters). It takes 4 months to reach 15 feet 6 inches (4.72 meters). Much of a season's temperature fluctuations are moderated in 7 feet (2 meters), and nearly all of a winter's worth in 15 feet (4.6 meters). The actual temperature difference in comparing 7 feet (2 meters) of Isolation Zone to 15 feet (4.6 meters) is quite small, amounting to only a few degrees per year, so the precise size of the Isolation Zone is not as important as simply using the principals involved.

In any event, no place on the actual structure should have any uninsulated underground portion within 10 to 14 feet (3 to 4 meters) along the conductive path to the nearest out-door surface; an effective Isolation Zone.

In addition to including good isolation for the home, a well isolated, large heat Storage Zone is essential. Yet there is considerable leeway in determining just how big the insulation/watershed umbrella must be. Certainly, the earth is quite forgiving once we have produced a Heat Storage Zone of a reasonable size. The idealized arrangement would necessarily be a compromise that also takes into consideration efficiency, cost, and ease of construction.

An umbrella which extends out about 20 feet (6 meters) in all possible directions would seem to be a reasonable compromise. Only the very top of the wall would have a conductive path less than about 25 feet (7.6 meters), so the greater body of earth under the umbrella, and next to the home can easily warm up to room temperature without interference from the out-door temperature extremes. This in fact has been the measured result in real PAHS homes.

If the home can be completely earth sheltered with 4 feet (1.2 meters) or so of earth, then there is enough room for a 2-foot (0.6-meter) thick Storage Zone on the roof. This portion of the earth cover can be very important because it will warm up to a slightly higher temperature than the walls, because of convection inside the home. And, it is easier to store heat that is already there than it is to move it someplace else for storage.

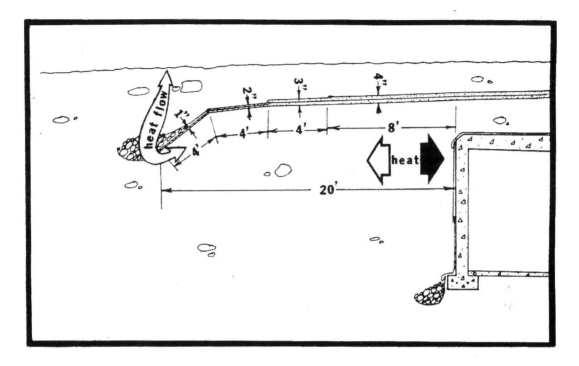

Figure 35 An idealized thermal storage arrangement makes possible a 20-foot storage zone around as much of the house as possible.

The idealized arrangement (Figure 35) would:

1. Extend the umbrella out 20 feet (6 meters) from the home in all directions. A circle would probably be the most practical configuration, angled down at its outer edge if possible.

2. If the home has the weight capacity to allow a small Storage Zone on the roof in addition to the usual 1.5 to 2 feet (0.46 to 0.6 meters) of moderating earth, then raise the umbrella up off of the roof as much as your structure will allow, while leaving a good Moderation Zone. Figure 35 shows 4 feet (1.2 meters) of total earth over; 2 feet (0.6 meters) of Moderation Zone, and 2 feet (0.6 meters) of Storage Zone.

3. The exposed surfaces of the home actually protrude through the insulation/ watershed umbrella, so the umbrella must abut the building in such a way that the building itself does not produce thermal short-circuits.

4. The umbrella itself has at least two layers of insulation sandwiched between at least three layers of plastic, taking into account all of the water drainage principles in Chapter 4. (Figure 18)

5. The insulation is tapered in 1 inch increments by going from 4 inches (10 centimeters) down to one inch (2.5 centimeters) out at the edge. The earth is forgiving enough that the tapering can be done in convenient 4-foot (1.2-meter) sections. 8 feet (2.4 meters) out at 4-inch (10-centimeter) thickness, then 4 feet (1.2 meters) at 3 inches (7.6 centimeters), then 4 feet at 2 inches (5 centimeters), and finally the last 4 feet at 1 inch (2.5 centimeters); for a total of 20 feet (6 meters). (Standard metric sizes of approximately the same size should work well too.)

This arrangement creates thermal isolation for a gigantic mass of earth without wrapping the whole thing in insulation. It sort of looks like a big ball with a hat on it. Heat will be absorbed and retrieved from this entire ball, even under the home, to the sides, and that portion of the ball which, as Storage Mass, is on the roof. Now, unless there is a major change in the annual balance of heat flow, a continuously comfortable climate can be produced as the heat flow through the structure establishes a new equilibrium temperature between the house and the Storage Zone. All of these things take place passively to become a built-in temperature that the very layout of the home and its components will maintain, for us, as an enjoyable temperature essentially forever.

Which Insulation?

Underground insulation has special requirements. Dirt is heavy, so we must choose an insulation that won't be mashed flat. It is primarily air inside the insulation that does the real insulating job. The plastic, fiberglass, or whatever is just there to hold that air still. So, insulation will not work if all the air gets squished out. That eliminates all but a handful of insulation types:

- Polyurethane, the brown spray-on type;
- Thermax®, the brown sheets with aluminum foil on them;
- Dow's blue Styrofoam board®; and
- white Expanded Polystyrene bead board.

Underground, even with the plastic protection, the insulation encounters water. Water is an excellent heat conductor, and any time the insulation soaks it up, it whittles away the thermal resistance, just as if it were being physically removed. Since the propaganda barrage for and against each type is quite intense, we undertook our own water absorption tests to determine what was really happening. Our results have been borne out by the experience of many others.

Polyurethane and Thermax® sheeting soak up water like a sponge and hang on to it tenaciously. The resulting R-value is practically worse than not having any insulation at all. (These same findings have also been reported on in several other texts.) In spite of the claims of some individuals (not the manufacturers,) the "orange-peel like skin" which forms on the spray-on polyurethane isn't anything like an underground waterproofing, and no one should attempt to use it that way. However, both are fine products that work very well ABOVE GROUND, such as on the exposed surfaces of the home, around windows etc. They can give you a higher "R" and some types of polyurethane can help reduce cold air infiltration, because they can be sprayed right into cracks.

Do not confuse "polyurethane" with "urea-formaldehyde" a product that is no longer in use in this country. It is a completely different product from polyurethane, with different properties. However, it should NOT be used underground either.

That leaves Styrofoam and bead board. (Here is where I'll contradict what some authors have said so please read carefully.)

1. Both products are very good and have a long track record of underground use.
2. Both must be protected from ultraviolet light.
3. Both have been consistently installed IMPROPERLY! Even being shown with improper installation in many texts.

Both type of insulations, the "closed cell" Styrofoam, blue Dow board and its clones, and the open cell bead board soak up water.

- Styrofoam—about 1 percent by volume.
- Bead board—about 2 percent by volume.

They have slightly different R-values.

- Styrofoam—5 and @ 1 percent moisture 4.95 (per inch thickness)
- Bead board—3.85 and @ percent moisture 3.77 (per inch thickness)

Therefore, to provide the same R-value the bead board must be slightly thicker, about 1.25 inches (3 centimeters), for the approximate equivalent to 1-inch of Styrofoam.

In actual use, with 4 or 5 inches (10 or 12 centimeters) of either of these, the loss in "R" is so small that any argument between the two is ridiculous; mostly advertising hype. At first, the bead board may appear to be the lesser product as it takes on more water. Yet it has been used for years as boat-dock floats, and they're still afloat. Because it has a smaller R-value per inch, it is usually put on a little thicker than Styrofoam, which increases its ability to resist water absorption.

It is the method of installation that is the most important consideration. Both water figures are derived by submerging them. But, both will DRAIN DRY, and regain their former resistances. In the past, these have been glued to the side of the concrete and water-soaked by a river of water pouring down over them. Even clay backfill has been used against them, sealing them up so that they would fill to overflowing; then people complain about the "loss in R."

If they are installed properly, as in an umbrella, fitted with the proper drainage and plastic shingles, whatever water does manage to trickle through the first layer of plastic quickly runs down to the drain gutter, not stopping to soak into anything. And if a little did? So what! It'll drain away a little later anyway.

No product should be installed improperly, and insulation installed without drainage is definitely improper. This includes BOTH types.

Two excellent products—both can serve you well.

But how do you decide? Figure out how much R-value you want, say about 20 (4 hr-m2-°C/kcal) on the roof (and more in very cold climates), calculate how many inches it would take of each (about 4 inches (10 centimeters) for Styrofoam, and 5 inches (12 centimeters) for bead board). Then count the cost of each. (Cost seems to answer most questions anyway.)

For most people, cost becomes the overriding factor. In most cases the bead board "cost per R" is much less. Therefore, on that basis I recommend bead board as the preferred product. Also, there are more manufacturers of bead board than there are of the other useable types. Their close proximity to the building site can cut transportation costs.

In a full PAHS design, one will use about a half a semi-truck load or more. Therefore, wholesale prices are generally available so as to make the PAHS method more cost effective as well as providing superior performance.

There is one other factor to take into consideration when trying to determine which insulation to use: CFC's or Chlorofluorocarbons. These CFCs have been identified as the substance which is most the responsible for the destruction of the Earth's ozone layer.

When the blue Down Styrofoam and its clones are manufactured, the basic plastic of the insulation is filled with these CFCs as its polystyrene base is extruded. The reason is that the CFCs have a higher R-value than plain air. It is extruded so that the tighter surface will retain the CFCs better.

White bead board is "expanded polystyrene." Tiny little beads of the base plastic, polystyrene, are blown up larger using hot steam, and molded into large blocks of insulation 2 feet thick, 4 feet wide, and 16 feet long (0.6 meters thick, 1.2 meters wide, and 4.8 meters long). Then this large block is dried. As the steam evaporates, it is replaced with plain old air. No CFCs are used at all. When dry, a hot wire is used to cut the large block into standard sizes.

Generally speaking, most any foam type of insulation which sports an R factor greater than bead board uses the CFCs to accomplish this. I have yet to see convincing evidence to indicate that the long term use of CFC laden insulation will not eventually lose its effectiveness because of CFC loss. Certainly, whenever the insulation gets wet, much of the CFCs would be displaced by the water. In an umbrella the water has a drainage path, and is generally kept quite dry. That is a plus for prolonging the life of the insulation. When the CFCs either leak out, or are pushed out by water, upon drying out, the replacement substance will be air.

While there may not be much air under the Moderation Zone, there is certainly enough to keep earthworms alive, and thus enough to provide air as the replacement gas for lost CFCs. I have also not seen any evidence that would suggest that the CFCs are harmless in the soil either.

The time frame which we would expect a good PAHS home to last is considerably longer than any other use for the products. Therefore, my choice is bead board. No CFCs, no possibility of the loss of insulating gas, its far cheaper in most instances, is more readily available, and is easier on the environment, both locally and globally.

The Warm and the Cool of It – Thermal Breaks

The basic insulation configuration is easy to comprehend and build but there are difficult places that take a little thinking. If we view the home in late winter, and label the portions of the earth, house, etc., either warm or cold, then we can determine where insulation should be. Wherever something warm and something cool come together, use insulation in between. Such insulation is called a THERMAL BREAK. For example: below the insulation umbrella (during a cold winter,) it is warm. Above, it's cold. The umbrella is bent down, as it follows the contour of the earth, wherever it nears openings in the earth for windows, doors and so on. Whatever sticks out through the umbrella must not become a thermal short circuit from the inside to the outside. It must be insulated, and its insulation protected from water just like in the umbrella.

Difficulties may also occur because of the order of construction necessary for getting the job done. For example: where a retaining wall attaches to the house there MUST be a thermal break; the wall will be cold and the home will be warm. Thermal breaks consist of insulation which is inserted between warm and cool things to prevent conductive losses that will short-circuit the other insulation arrangements. When the umbrella is installed, the earth behind the wall will probably be warm. If the wall is not insulated ON THE BACK, then a short circuit (a very big one) will exist right smack in the middle of the Storage Zone. (Figure 36)

Just wait until you tell the boys to insulate the BACK of the retaining wall… you thought you had problems convincing them to PUT IN thermal breaks in the first place!

Remember the basic principles of conduction? (Figure 35-A) These are some of the types of thermal breaks that have appeared in various publications. Putting in thermal breaks is certainly commendable, but of how much use are they when an alternate path is so quickly taken by the moving heat? If we think of the structure as a whole, including the earth, rather than just its parts, we'll be more effective in designing useful parts that will not be made useless by some other part. Figure 36b details how these should be made, recognizing heat's habit of sneaking into an unsuspected path of least resistance.

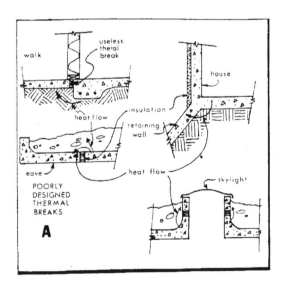 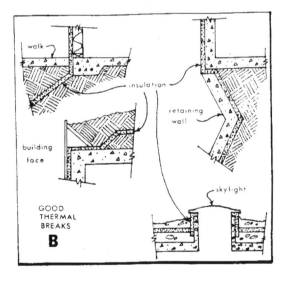

Figure 36 A & B Properly designed thermal breaks do not have thermal short circuits around them.

The self-supporting retaining wall is certainly easier to insulate than one which requires steel bars through the thermal break to keep it from falling over. It is difficult enough because the bottom of the wall is so close to the exposed surface, with its conductive path going right under the wall. One could take the wall down deeper, but in most cases this would be more costly than it is worth. Therefore, do what you can to reduce the over-all surface area of exposure, and make the conductive paths as long as you can. Curving the insulation under (Figure 36-B) is one of several ways to do this, especially up close to the house.

Most home designers, architects and engineers alike, tend to design things the way they have been designing them, because "that's the way it's done." Humans are creatures of habit. Attaching a cold retaining wall, even with only the steel rebar connecting it to a warm house is a thermal blunder. There are many types of retaining walls that won't fall over without being held up by the house. Just extend the umbrella between the house and the retaining wall, making sure that any exposed part of the umbrella is protected from sunlight and surface damage.

The order of construction will have a bearing on the exact design. This thermal break between the wall and the house must be put in when the wall is being built. The back of the retaining wall must be insulated before backfilling that wall. However, the umbrella proper, which will abut the insulation on the back of the wall, will be installed half way through the job of backfilling the whole building.

Installing the Umbrella

Backfill ALL BUT the last two feet (60 centimeters) of earth over the entire building, leaving a 4- or 5-foot (1.2- or 1.5-meter) deep depression (measuring from the final earth surface) out where the outer edge of the umbrella will be, if practical. Shape the earth gently as it curves down under windows and doors, always paying attention to the expected water flow. Now is when you must remember to put in all the sloping gutters, so that you can build the complete umbrella drainage system of Chapter 3.

Then pick a day when the wind isn't blowing, otherwise you'll have insulation and plastic blown all over Texas and half of Arkansas!

There are two proven ways of constructing the umbrella. The first is to lay out the umbrella, one layer at a time in its final location. If the slope of the backfill is just shallow enough to produce good water runoff, this method works well. One problem has been that the workers keep falling down! Yes, the plastic is very slippery; I've fallen many times myself.

A second method is to construct the umbrella a little ways away from its final location. Lay out each component in the proscribed manner and hold the various parts in place using small squares of duct tape. Usually, only the layers of plastic out on the end need be taped together every 4 to 6 feet (2 meters). Do not run tons of tape across the whole thing. The tape is only a temporary holding device during construction, and you don't want the water drainage to be blocked by tape, or the pocket book to shrink because of over-zealous use of tape.

Use the largest pieces of plastic you are able to. Generally, 20-foot (6-meter) wide plastic is available. Lay out a 20-foot (6-meter) section along with a 10-foot (3-meter) section to form a gutter on the outer end, and 2 or 3 feet (0.6 or 1.2 meter) shingle overlap. The upper side will either be abutted to an exposed, insulated portion of the house, or will connect to another part of the umbrella, depending upon where it is located (Figure 18).

Lay out the first layer of insulation. Remember that it varies in thickness (1 inches (2.5 centimeters) on the outer end to about 4 inches (10 centimeters) next to the house). However, this first layer is about half of that. So lay out 2 inches (5 centimeters) next to the house, for the first 12 feet (3.6 meters). (The exact distances are chosen by the width of the insulation board; do not cut the insulation to match any arbitrary number.) The last 8 feet (2.4 meters) is laid out with 1-inch (2.5-centimeter) board.

Then put down the second plastic layer. It should start from the same place as the first sheet of plastic near the house, and should extend out beyond the last insulation board as in Figure 19. Position the insulation boards tightly together so that there is little or no space between the boards. Once the second layer of plastic is in place, and taped, the whole thing will stay together reasonably well.

If the shape of the umbrella dictates that boards be cut, for convenience, small portions of the insulation may be overlapped with each other, but generally this is not necessary.

Next place the second layer of insulation. Once again, pay attention to the thickness as in Figure 35. (Note the layout of Figure 18.) Each of the boards in the top layer is placed over the cracks between the boards of the lower layer. This prevents the dirt of the Moderation Zone from pressing down to form a short circuit, pushing the insulation to the side.

The third layer of plastic is then installed, and held in place by using small squares of duct tape out on the end where the layers of plastic come together.

Once these large sections of the umbrella are assembled, two or three workers are able to grab the edge near the house and drag the whole assemblage up into position. Once in position, several shovel loads of dirt can be thrown on top to help hold things together. Minor adjustments can then be made by one worker while the other puts drainage gravel out on the end, and between the plastic layers on the end for the umbrella drainage system.

Before backfilling, stand back and look at the entire umbrella. Visualize in your mind where the water is going to flow after it seeps through the Moderation Zone. Make sure there will be no puddles, or lakes formed AFTER THE BACKFILL SETTLES. Make sure that the connection to the home is proper. And make sure that there are no big gaps or thermal short circuits.

Also, remember to allow enough insulation on the house so that after the backfill settles it will not leave any bare spots on the house itself. The "warm" house is insulated where it is ABOVE ground (Figure 74), and a "cold" retaining wall is insulated BELOW ground. (Figure 34) When the umbrella is complete, backfill the last two feet (60 centimeters) of earth over it.

If you drive right over the umbrella, with no earth on it, you will wish you hadn't. Push or dump a 10- to 12-inch (25- or 30-centimeter) layer of protective earth onto the umbrella BEFORE you drive on it. Usually this can be done in "lifts" in the standard excavating manner, working your way from the outside towards the center. This is where all the care of installation, as described in the previous chapter, must be taken. Remember, the biggest enemy that insulation and plastic seem to have is people!

In some cases, you can lay down some sheets of plywood for the equipment to drive on, but this should be in addition to the foot (30-centimeter) of earth cover that is pushed ahead of the equipment.

The first few inches may also be backfilled using clay, as described back in Chapter 4. Experience has shown that the dirt in the Moderation Zone may slide right off the umbrella, if the ground it is laid on is very steep. This has happened in some cases to homes built in the very wet climate of the Pacific Northwest portion of North America. The solution is to either keep the slope small, or put down a fabric mat such as landscapers often use to hold the soil until a good buildup of grass roots can be grown in the Moderation Zone. Once that is accomplished, the arrangement has proven to be quite stable.

Cost Comparisons

Everybody wants to do cost comparisons between the PAHS method and others. Is the PAHS method the cheapest way to go: definitely not. Mike Oehler's $50 and Up Underground House Book certainly presents a very inexpensive way to build. And the PAHS method certainly will work well, when added to Mike's thoughtful designs.

Will the usual PAHS design cost more than a conventional aboveground home? Probably. Is longevity, and a permanently comfortable environment, in a low maintenance structure that is much safer from tornados, fires and many other natural disasters, and in harmony with the Earth's environment more valuable than a stick-built home? It depends upon where you place the "value." Living with the hobos in the bushes by the railroad track is certainly cheaper, but is it as comfortable?

If we compare a common PAHS home, with a conventional underground home what do we find? The roof of a conventional underground home usually has the same amount of insulation over it (Figure 27) as a PAHS home; about 4 inches (10 centimeters). The conventional arrangement also has a layer of high-priced waterproofing under the insulation. Rain water soaks the insulation, and as a result there is a definite loss of thermal resistance.

The Umbrella on the other hand, keeps that same amount of insulation dry, as well as the earth underneath it. Integral waterproofing agents are used in the concrete, along with a single layer vapor barrier. Fours layer of plastic altogether. So, on the roof the cost comparison is between a small amount of concrete additive, with four layers of plastic for the umbrella, and one very thick layer of expensive layer of waterproofing.

For the earth shelter portions of the building, the conventional method would have 16 board feet (0.037 meters) of wet insulation and 8 square feet (0.74 square meters) of waterproofing. The umbrella would have 56 board feet (0.13 meters) of insulation and 64 square feet (6 square meters) of plastic per running foot (30 centimeters) of wall.

If we compare a 64 by 24 foot home with 8 foot walls, the result is 1,536 square feet of roof area (143 square meters), and with three earth sheltered walls, of 8 by 112 = 896 square feet (83 square meters) For a total surface of 2,432 square feet (226 square meters) of surface to be waterproofed in the conventional manner.

Now as soon as I mention a price, the price will change, so don't count on these prices, but I'll use them so that proportionally you can get an idea of how things work. If you can get the waterproofing at about $1 per square foot without counting labor and waste, (which is a very good price, and easy to figure with). Therefore, the waterproofing should cost about $2,432.00. If the plastic runs about $0.02 per square feet and the insulation runs $0.15 per board feet then the umbrella should cost around $936.24. If you subtract that from the cost of the expensive waterproofing yields $1,495.76 left to spend on something else over what would have been spent in the conventional method.

With all of the variables in both cost of materials, labor and waste, and the differing economies my readers worldwide encounter it's impossible to determine here in Montana what your costs will be where you are. But I've included this comparison so that you can get an idea of what can be done. So if you get a bid with an outrageous price, you will be able to compare the bid to the figures you can generate yourself by this comparison.

In general it is safe to say that a PAHS home should not cost any more than the equivalently sized conventional underground. The umbrella takes far less labor than conventional waterproofing. So, a good builder should be able to produce underground homes that are less costly than an equivalently size stick built above ground home. Other builders have achieved that goal, and yours should too.

Applications

Did I say that your bungalow had to be a geodesic dome, or even round? While there are many fine advantages in using these shapes, the best reasons are primarily structural. While there are some thermal advantages with these basic shapes, thoughtful design can easily over-come any handicaps and maybe uncover some advantages to other shapes as well.

The principles outlined above give us a practical, easily applied method of inexpensive heat storage for very long periods. The trick is to use it without messing it up. Keeping it simple is a good axiom that reduces mistakes and helps us apply these basics properly.

Immersing the house in this newly warmed earth is the easiest way of moving heat in and out, but is by no means the only way. Read on. There's a lot more to come.

Notes:

Chapter 6 – What Goes Up

Passive annual heat storage is in reality a combination of heat flow types. First the radiant sunshine comes into the home, with the home itself being the solar collector. But then much of this heat will not go directly into the heat saving earth. It must be carried there by another method of moving heat around: CONVECTIVE HEAT FLOW.

Many interesting and useful processes will become available to us with a proper understanding of convection. We'll be able to make the heat move itself to where we want it, when we need it. It can power a fresh air system to keep us comfortable, even make that fresh air WARM in the WINTER, and COOL in the SUMMER.

But, in order to accomplish these fine jobs, we first need a good working knowledge of convective heat flow in the practical world.

Convective Heat Flow

Convection is the familiar one. "Hot air rises," is the way most people put it. As familiar as people may be with convection, some absolutely atrocious set-ups have been built in an attempt to use convective heat flow, with disastrous results. A down-to-earth understanding of convection will, in our underground homes, provide the missing link that is necessary for getting our incoming sunbeams really down to earth.

Convection is one of the most sensitive types of heat flow. It is very sensitive to its environment, and may be easily over-shadowed by the action of other principles, affecting how and where heat is moved. This is especially so in air because you cannot readily see exactly what may be happening, because you cannot see the air. That is in most cities you still can't see it.

Therefore, when its action is over-shadowed, we may not be aware of it, or even suspect it. That makes the design job all that much more difficult. An everyday example illustrates this "over-shadowing": Hot air rises. It rises outdoors just as much as it will indoors. Why then, is it cold on mountain tops? Shouldn't it be hot? Yes, more than just one principle is involved. Principles, unlike laws, can be over-shadowed by other principles so as to produce an entirely different result from what one might have expected. If you design your house upon the assumption that "hot air always rises," you could find yourself living uncomfortably in a very cold or hot house.

To be more precise, hot air doesn't really rise, so much as it floats. If all of the air in a home is heated to the same temperature, it simply gets hot, and goes nowhere. The hot air that rises is actually any air that is warmer than the surrounding air, and the cool air which descends must only be cooler than the warm air which displaces it. Convection takes place even in what we would normally call, "hot air," or "cold air." In fact, air masses of different temperatures will tend to seek their own levels, hot air on top, warm air in the middle and cool air at the bottom, just as a submarine will adjust its depth by making itself heavier or lighter.

People often forget that the cool air must descend. If the cool air is not allowed to descend, then the hot air cannot rise to replace it. While that may seem like a silly thing to be reminded of, a close examination of many solar homes will reveal that a proper place has been made for hot air to go, but no provision has been made for the cool air. The usual result is stagnation with places that are too hot or cold to be pleasant.

This is significant because many people have built homes expecting heat storage by convection, when in fact they were running, not warm air as they had expected, but cool air into their storage bins.

Closed Convective Loops

Take a close look at Figure 37. Note its essential parts:
1. A container that allows the free flow of air within itself.
2. A heat source on one SIDE, (heat input).
3. A heat sink (a cooler place for heat to go) on the other SIDE.

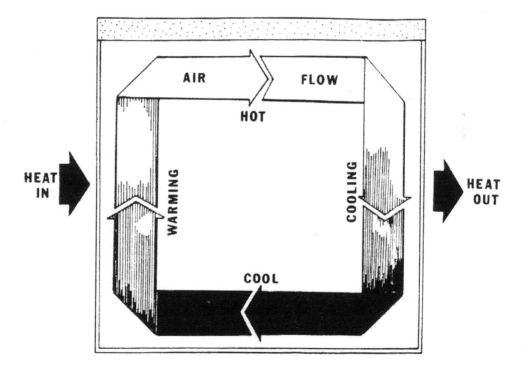

Figure 37 An unconfined closed convective loop with a container full of air, a heat source, and a heat sink.

John Hait

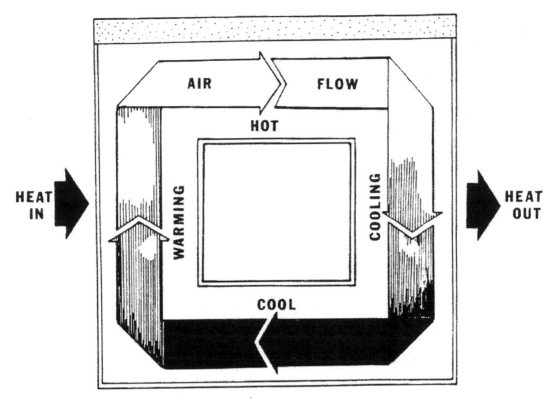

Figure 38 A confined closed convection loop that works just like Figure 37.

The heat, entering on the left warms the air so that it will expand and rise. This action pushes the cooler air back and down, as it sinks to the floor, and the ceiling warms up. If that heat had nowhere to go stagnation would occur with the warm air being gathered at the top, and the room would be heated gradually, from the top down. If on the other-hand, the back wall has a place for heat to go, a heat sink, then the warm air which reaches it will cool off and settle to the floor. The continuous action of heat coming in on the one side, and heat going out on the other side, causes a continuous flow of air, and thus a continuous flow of heat, a convective loop.

As long as there is no interference with any of the three essential parts, the loop will continue to pump heat from the warm side to the cool side. This action is quite efficient in spite of the high R-value of air, or more precisely, because of its high R-value, and air's ability to move so easily. These convective loops will be established even in very small places, between the panes of glass of a dual-pane window for example. That's why the R-value (1/R) of windows doesn't improve very much when the thickness of the air space is increased beyond ¾ of an inch (2

102

centimeters) or so. The convective loop is established, and the space in between is effectively bypassed. In fact, one of the primary methods of creating insulation is to provide something to hold the air still so its high R can be used. Fiberglass insulation is an excellent example.

A Place for Everything

A number of fine convective loop solar collection systems have been devised. Basically, the various parts of the loop are designed to provide for a single operation, so things don't get too complicated and probably out of control. (See Figure 39) In this arrangement, called a "Thermal-syphon," the place where we want the heat to go, the box of rocks, is put at the top of the loop.

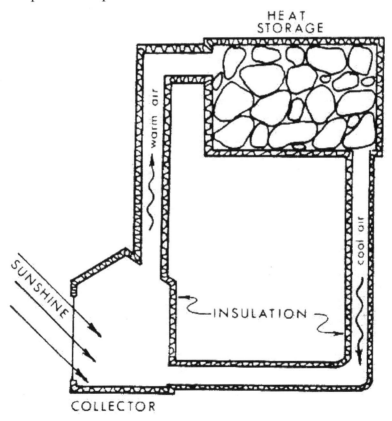

Figure 39 The thermal syphon is a closed confined convective loop with an insulated heat storage sink on top.

Why is it put up there? Because that's where it's warmest. If the storage box were put at the bottom instead of the top, the cool air would descend into it, and it would be a "cold storage box." (Surely you say no one would put the "heat storage box" on the bottom. Well take a close look at the designs for many of the "double envelope" homes that have appeared in the popular press recently!)

The two pipes linking the collector to the storage box are insulated, this is important because heat must be prevented from entering the cool pipe or leaving the warm pipe causing a reverse flow. The cool air has a "place to go," and it will go exactly where we want it to. Note what happens when the sun goes down. The heat input has stopped. The warm air will be trapped at the top of the loop because it has nowhere else to rise to. Since the bottom of the loop is already filled with cold air the loop will grind to a stagnate halt, and the precious heat will be trapped inside. If, however, the storage zone and the collector were at the same level, the warm air would have a place to go, so the loop would reverse itself and pump the heat right back out. (Figure 42)

Note that the natural balance of heat flow has been altered, in the thermal syphon, in that it has been made easier for the heat to enter than to escape. Keep this in mind when we get to the chapter on adjusting the deep earth temperature.

Envelopes with Windows in them (Homes)

Everyone gets envelopes in the mail with windows in them, usually bills. An improperly designed envelope home, whether underground or not, will bring in a lot more windowed envelopes than it would with a correct layout of windows and envelope.

Figure 40 is a typical double envelope design that has appeared in a number of magazines, a basic design that has often been applied to underground houses. The claim is made that the heat is "stored in the crawl space underneath the house." Is it? Look closely at its convective loop. Where is the cold air going? Isn't the so-called storage area actually the coolest part of the loop? How effective can such an arrangement be?

The reports on their operation are often rather interesting, such as this one: "There is no detectable air flow, but we're sure it's working rather well." I would suggest that if there is "no detectable air flow" then there probably isn't a significant amount of air flow, and certainly the colder temperatures that are reported to be in the crawl-space show that there is not a significant amount of heat being stored. Some reports in the popular press are even more ridiculous. They have the undetectable imaginary air flow going in all sorts of directions sometimes even blowing against itself. Rather, the most common result of such an arrangement is simply stagnation. Heat storage built into the attic would certainly be more appropriate.

The convective loop requires a heat input AND a heat output in order to keep working. To force such an arrangement to work at least a little bit, fans are used to make happen what would have happened naturally if it had been designed right in the first place. Even with fans, the entire body of air, the whole thing, must be heated up warmer than the storage zone by an appreciable amount before any heat will be stored at all. When the sun goes down and the outdoor temperature cools off, the windows become the heat SINK, (a cool place for heat to go). So the interior, and the crawl space (if you have any heat stored at all,) become the source. Now the convective loop reverses direction, pumping the heat back out. This reverse flow, unless prevented by closing off the air flow passages, or insulating the glass at night, is worsened by the addition of, what would ordinarily be considered a good idea, a super-insulated north wall!

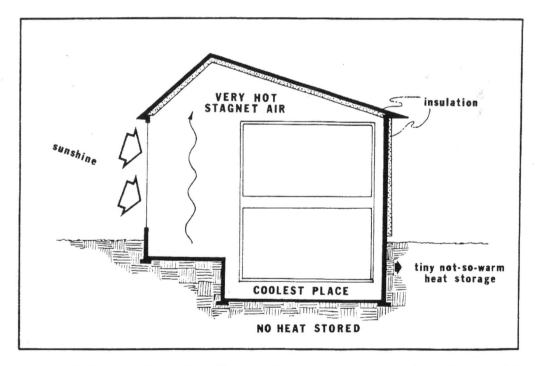

Figure 40 An improperly designed but popular convective envelope home. In spite of the claims, very little heat will actually be stored in the earth underneath the house.

Why would a super-insulated north wall make it work even WORSE? Because the convective loop requires both an input and an output in order to keep working. If the DAYTIME output is shut off by super-insulating the back wall the loop will STOP. When the loop stops, so does the storing of what little heat was blowing its way into the crawl space. However, this occurs only during the DAYTIME when the sun is shining. At night an output path is readily available and because the sink is now ABOVE, or at the very least, level with the new source, what stored heat there is, is pumped outside much more rapidly than it was pumped in! It is in effect a REVERSE THERMAL SYPHON.

Over the long haul, this arrangement would have a tendency to "store cold," That is, it would continuously cool itself off. Such a house would also tend to be hot in the summer and cold in the winter, with wide daily temperature fluctuations.

Now that I've raised the ire of envelope enthusiasts everywhere, notice why these actual problems have not been so obvious. A great number of things are usually included in each design that clouds the basics of convective heat flow. Remember I said that convection was sensitive? Insulation on the windows at night, fans, conduction, the sun shining all the way inside and over-all super-insulation makes them work better than many "conventional" homes. But so-called "conventional above-ground homes" are really a poor standard. The only viable standard is one that requires no commercial energy at all.

Scores of theoretical arguments have arisen because envelope homes have made some improvement, but a full understanding of why they work, or don't work, will allow us to sort out the reasons, and design accordingly. A well thought-out convective loop should be the first consideration in designing any home, and the concept of using a double envelope should not be discarded off hand. Convection is very efficient. However, it may be working for you or against you.

Envelope Convective Loops

Take a look at Figure 41. It is an earth-BERMED home. That means that earth has been piled up around its sides, but it does not have an earth sheltered roof. In place of a massive, heat-storing, heat-moderating roof is a light weight, non-heat-storing, super-insulated roof. Often such homes are also called earth sheltered. Many readers may wish to design earth-bermed homes. The principles of Passive Annual Heat Storage apply just as much to them as to their fully covered cousins. The reduced surface area available for moving heat into and out of the Storage Zone does make this type of home a little harder to work with. However, the pioneer in Passive Annual Heat Storage should have little trouble applying the principles and producing a fine, well operating home.

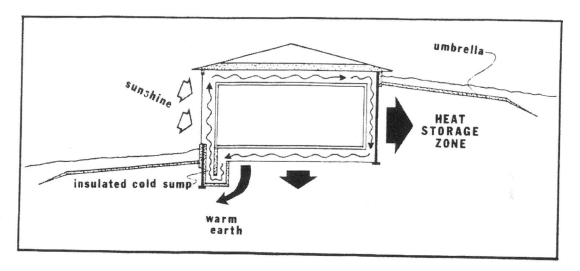

Figure 41 A properly designed envelope home will store gigantic amounts of heat. Here an insulation/watershed umbrella is used along with an insulated cold sump to prevent conduction from canceling the effect of a properly designed convective loop.

I am using this type of home here because it makes convective heat flow a little easier to understand. An earth sheltered roof would also store and return heat, but it is easy to heat with convection because it's on the top. The rest of the earth is more difficult to get the warm air down to. This explanation will help you understand how that may be accomplished.

This design has a heat input, and a heat storage sink, (a heat output when the sun is shining). There is a place for the hot air to go, and a place for the cold air to go. Everywhere we want heat to move in and out of storage is located in at least the WARM parts of the loop. The cold part of the loop is in the "cold sump." and it must be large enough to contain the expected amount of cold air that will be gathered there. Also, it must be insulated from the warm conductive surroundings. With this arrangement we will actually be storing heat UNDER the floor.

The interior of the home would have very little effect on the loop during the daytime, summertime or whenever you are collecting those golden rays. Therefore, at INPUT TIME, the internal envelope is really of little value unless the air temperature is made uncomfortably high. (Raising the temperature is a method often used to force the old inefficient ones to work.)

At night however…

If any of the basic principles that make a convective loop work are removed, the heat flow will stop. First of all, cold air will settle into the cold sump and prevent reverse flow. However, extreme cold can overpower this and turn the loop on, anyway. The heat output may be prevented by covering the windows with insulation or by having the air flow stopped, and then the loop will be broken. There is, however, some heat loss that will be sustained by the interior. Therefore, heat MUST be allowed to enter it. Also, the windows may be placed below the level of storage. The sinking cold air will then fill these collectors and trap all the heat above it as with a thermal syphon.

Since these methods of preventing night and cloudy day losses work even without the interior envelope, good air circulation can accomplish the same job much more cheaply and easily. However, the raised floor has additional comfort advantages so you may wish to retain it.

This particular drawing (Figure 41) also gives us an idea of how the heat storage principles discussed earlier may be applied to a wide variety of home designs, and are by no means confined to the full earth shelter.

The Open Convection Loop

Now let's consider what can be done if the convective loop is modified as in Figure 42. This is called the open loop. Note that it requires the source, sink and connecting pipes to be separate. An open loop system will not work in a big open room, or if a door or window is open. As before, the heat input (sunshine) heats the air on the left, and the heat sink removes the heat allowing the cool air to fall through the right hand pipe. Rather than recycling the same old air through the system, the open loop takes a new breath of air as long as heat is moving in the loop, (either into or out of storage). If part of the loop is a living space, then we will have a continuous supply of fresh air whenever heat is moving into or out of the house. Now we have a solar powered ventilation system that works even when the sun isn't shining, since it is also powered by stored solar heat.

In order to isolate the system from the outdoor weather the heat exchanger will warm the winter air, cool the summer air, and allow the convective loop to function at any temperature we like. Without it, operating temperatures may not be in the range where we feel comfortable.

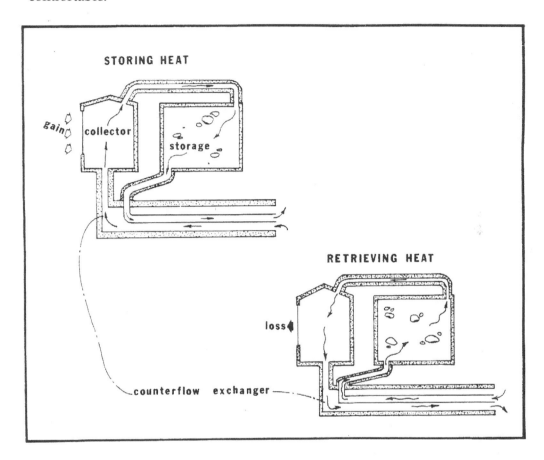

Figure 43 An open convective loop requires its parts (source, sink, and storage) to be separate like the confined loop of Figure 38. Plus it uses a counterflow heat exchanger to allow the stale air to be replaced with nice, fresh air.

Counterflow Heat Exchangers

Heat exchangers basically move heat from a warm gas or liquid, like the indoor stale air (in the winter) and put it into another fluid like cold outdoor fresh air so it can enter at a comfortable temperature, very near the temperature that the stale air was at when it left.

Figure 43 shows two types of heat exchangers, parallel flow and counterflow. In the parallel flow, as the name suggests, the air is moving in the same direction in both pipes. Heat will pass through the walls of the interior pipe from the hot air to the cold air. The cold air is warmed up, and the hot air is cooled off, and their temperatures meet in the middle coming out the other end, WARM.

The counterflow heat exchanger on the other hand, has its fluids (gas or liquid in either or both tubes) traveling in OPPOSITE directions. Once again, the hot one cools, and the cold one warms up. But, when the cold one reaches the other end of the pipe it sees, not a warm fluid that has already been cooled off, but a hot one that hasn't had a chance to cool yet, and the hot one sees a cold fluid at its other end. Note Figure 43. When the fluid which is supplying heat is HOT, the one receiving heat can get HOT. But if the source fluid were to lose its temperature in the process, as with the parallel flow heat exchanger, how could it make the destination fluid anything but WARM? This way, the HOT ONE comes out COLD, and the COLD ONE comes out HOT.

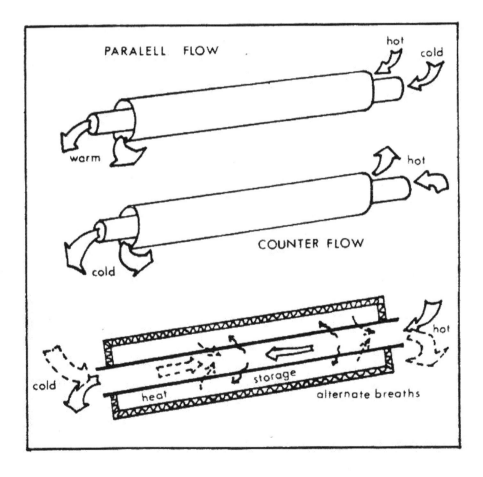

Figure 43 Counterflow and Parallel-flow heat exchangers. The bottom illustration is a counterflow, "camel's nose", heat exchanger.

The counterflow heat exchanger has one end of the machine at the highest temperature, and the other end at the lowest temperature, while the heat carrying fluids are going in opposite directions. Therefore, the addition of a counterflow heat exchanger to the convective loop in a home will moderate the incoming air to a comfortable temperature since it tends to keep it warm on one side and cool on the other. In this way it allows the main convective loop to concentrate on storing and retrieving heat and keeps it isolated from the outdoor temperatures that would have an adverse effect on its operation.

Counterflow heat exchangers are becoming popular. A number of them are on the market and they can be made to work rather well (although they are not always as efficient as we would like). Coupled with our new massive earth heat storage techniques, these simple heat exchangers can provide heat movement both into and out of storage, year around (ROOM TEMPERATURE) fresh air, eliminate trapped indoor pollution, and even provide an excellent means of adapting underground heat control to above ground homes. However, another type of heat exchanger is far less expensive and at the same time will provide us with a better tool for accomplishing all these neat tasks.

Notes:

Chapter 7 – Earth Tube Ventilation

Earth tubes are excellent heat exchangers. As in the heat exchangers discussed in the previous chapter, earth tubes will either warm or cool the air that enters them. Actually, the air which enters is moderated to nearly match the temperature of the earth around them.

Basically, an earth tube is a pipe between 4 and 18 inches (10 and 46 centimeters) in diameter and at least 60 feet (18 meters), but usually 100 or more feet (30 meters) long. They are buried in the ground, with one end inside the home, and the other outside. They can be made of almost any kind of pipe. Thin-wall PVC is a favorite, since it has all its seams sealed to prevent unwanted things like roots and moisture from entering, and it is relatively inexpensive.

The Camel's Nose

Interestingly, there is quite a similarity between the heat exchange function of an earth tube and the operation of a camel's nose! No kidding, a camel's nose has a lot to do with earth tubes.

Maybe you haven't studied a camel's nose very closely. But it is his big and unusual nose that gives him his unique ability to go for long periods of time without water, and to maintain a constant body temperature even in extreme climates. The camel's nose is a very efficient counterflow heat exchanger.

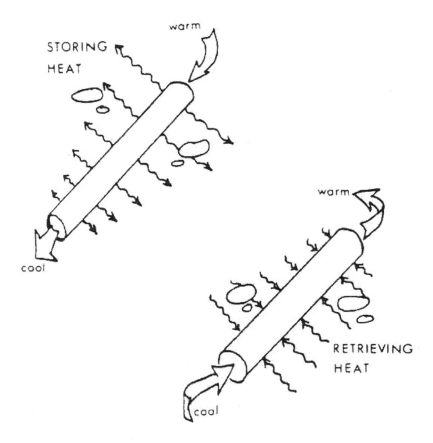

Figure 44 An earth tube can operate as a counterflow heat exchanger, which like a camel's nose, stores heat between successive breaths of air going in opposite directions.

Unlike most man made heat exchange, the heat transfer in a camel's nose occurs not between two fluids traveling in opposite directions, but from a single fluid (air) into thermal storage (the passages of the nose) when he is inhaling, and back out again when he exhales. Whether it is warm or cold outside, the air enters the lungs at about body temperature, because the heat is stored in the nose between successive breaths and returned to wherever it came from.

Earth tubes are also very effective at storing and retrieving heat just like a camel's nose. (Figure 44) And like a camel, a home should be kept at a constant "body" temperature regardless of the weather. All we must do is make the earth tubes breathe.

The Usual (Old Fashioned) Earth Tube

Before we make earth tubes "breathe," let's look at some of the common configurations, determine why they work the way they do, and how we can improve their operation.

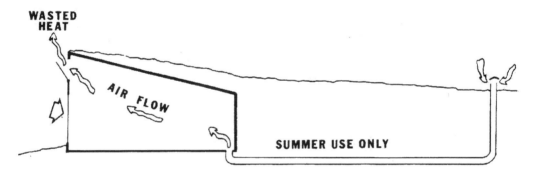

Figure 45 The usual (old type) earth tube arrangement must dump heat in order to power itself.

Usually a single earth tube, is used, and laid in the ground with the thought that the air will be cooled by the earth. (Figure 45) That will happen IF the air is WARMER than the earth, but if the air is colder than the earth, the air will be warmed. Since many people mistakenly believe that the earth must be cool all the time, they often call them "cool tubes," and expect them to work that way.

An interesting example of such an earth tube is incorporated in an early earth shelter here in Montana, (not the Geodome). Its tube is 8 inches (20 centimeters) in diameter and 130 feet (40 meters) long, laid fairly level, and shaped similar to Figure 45, parallel to the northern subterranean wall. In the SUMMER the hot outside air is cooled to about 65°F (18°C) and in the WINTER the frigid Montana air is warmed to about 65°F (18°C).

In both cases the air temperature is moderated by the earth, very similar to the action of the moderation zone on the top of the house, only the latter works by conduction through the earth layer and the former works by conduction through the pipe. Nevertheless, fresh air enters the house at a nearly constant temperature, all year around.

But why isn't it a cool tube? Why doesn't it enter the home at 45°F (7°C) which is the deep-earth temperature here in Montana? Because (as Chapter 2) explains, the earth around the home has been climatized to 65°F (18°C). True, this two story home does NOT have an insulation umbrella; nevertheless, the earth is still climatized to a new temperature. It is just a bit lower than it would be if the umbrella were there. In this case 65°F.

The configuration of Figure 45, which is the usual layout that is pictured in most 'how to do it' books, is really a WARM climate design. A COLD climate design would require quite a few changes.

The stale air should NOT be exhausted out the top. True, this could be powered by convection, but no provision is made to capture the valuable heat that would be lost in such an arrangement. A practical convectively operated earth tube can be made without throwing away such a tremendous amount of heat. Even an electric fan would not use as much energy as is wasted in this arrangement, especially in the wintertime. But don't throw away your sky-light just yet; it will come in handy when we get to adjusting the deep-earth temperature. In order to retrieve those billowing BTU's, we can utilize an open convective loop, a nice pair of earth tubes set up as counterflow heat exchangers, and even the underground heat storage as well, to do the trick.

Passive Earth Tube Ventilation

Take a gander at Figure 46. Here we have a breathing, open loop, convective powered, counterflow heat exchanged, earth tube ventilation system. (How's that for a mouth full?) Each of the basic parts of an open loop system is there. As with the designation of the various parts of the earth as to function (Storage Zone, Moderation Zone and the like) each part of the earth tube ventilation system has a separate function. First, a solar collector which is the heat source, namely the solar-heated earth-sheltered home itself. The heat sink is the deep-earth Storage Zone far back under the insulation umbrella. The top of the convective loop is just an extension of the earth tube. The counterflow heat exchanger is the pair of earth tubes which exit out the bottom of the loop.

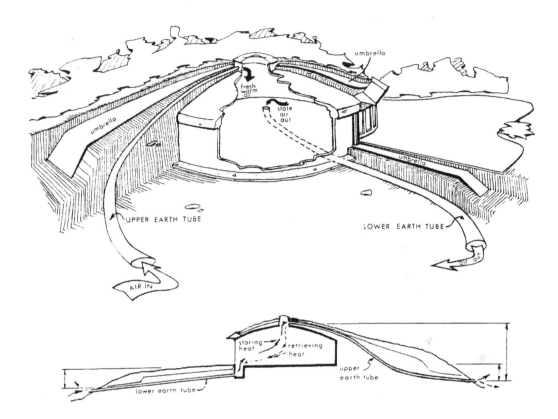

Figure 46 An open look, convectively-powered, "camel's nose," counterflow heat exchanged, earth tube ventilation system that stores and retrieves heat automatically while providing year-round fresh air, at room temperature.

The heat storage and retrieval section which is in the Storage Zone, MUST go downhill from the TOP of the house. Its tail end, and THE WHOLE LOWER PIPE, must continue to go downhill from about floor level. They constitute the counterflow heat exchange portion. (Compare Figures 46 & 42)

Breathing, How it Works

Whenever the temperature inside the house attempts to rise, the air will move into the upper tube, and will cool off, giving its heat to the earth in the Storage Zone. This gradually cooling air FALLS through the steep downhill, first portion, of the tube. In the lower portion of that same tube, the air will be adjusted gradually to nearly match the outdoor temperature. In the winter time, it will have cooled off. In the summer it will warm up. Thus, stale internal air is exhausted into the atmosphere.

However, without the second lower tube, no FRESH AIR could replace that which has been exhausted, unless you open a window, which is a completely unacceptable idea whenever it is either very cold or very hot outside. Thus the SECOND TUBE is there to moderate the incoming fresh air so it will enter at or near room temperature. The addition of this second tube is one of the greatest advances in earth tube technology. Even if the design you choose is not convection powered, every design should have a tube for incoming air, AND a tube for outgoing air.

Now the sun goes down, and slowly the interior begins to cool off. In the case of the earth home the interior cools very slowly. Whenever the indoor temperature attempts to fall, the air inside will contract, and it too will fall, right out the lower earth tube. Its temperature will be adjusted to meet the outdoor temperature (with some delay,) and fresh air will be sucked into the home through the upper tube. This air is moderated in the first portion of the tube, and then heated slightly more through the Storage Zone.

Thus earth tubes can be made to "breathe." One breath occurs whenever the indoor temperature attempts to rise, and the earth tubes store the excess heat in the earth. The other breath occurs whenever the indoor temperature attempts to fall, bringing heat from the earth back into the home. The over-all result is to tie the indoor temperature of the home more closely to the earth storage temperature while supplying fresh air at the same time. There are however, many details to which attention must be paid.

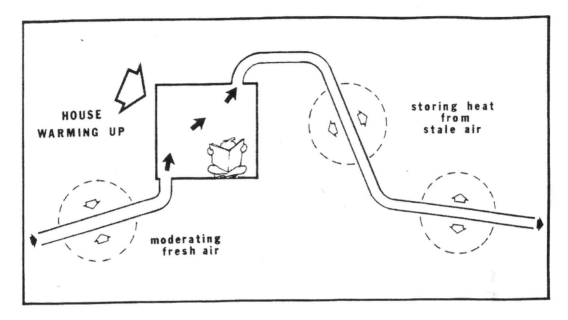

Figure 47 The heat storage "breath" stores excess heat in the earth, warming incoming winter air, while saving heat from outgoing stale air.

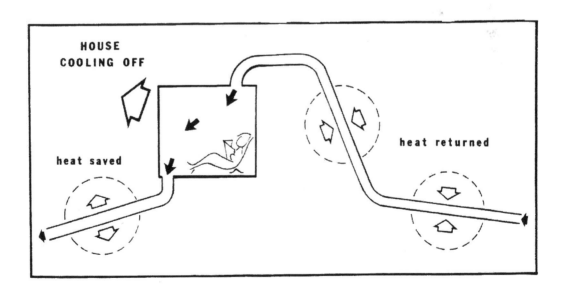

Figure 48 The heat retrieval "breath" warms incoming fresh winter air and adds extra needed heat from the Storage Zone. It also saves heat from the stale air being exhausted.

How Earth Tube Operation Is Affected by Length

Earth tubes have been constructed in lengths all the way from 30 feet to 130 feet (9 to 40 meters). The shorter ones tend to be more fussy to work with and give more trouble than do the longer ones. This is because of the effect of heat exchange on the temperature of the earth next to the tube. These dynamic effects heat flow are not generally noticed by the time the air reaches the end of a long tube, because longer tubes have more of an opportunity for heat exchange. There is much we can learn though from short tubes. So, short tubes are more fun, but long tubes work better. Let's see why.

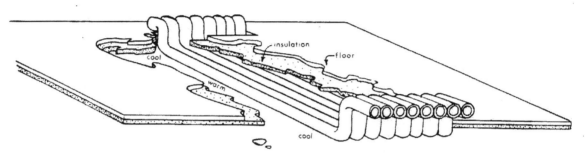

Figure 49 Using short multiple pipes in an attempt to replace longer ones didn't work as well as expected.

The earth environment is dynamic. It is NOT STATIC. This is evidenced by the report in the July/August 1982, (page 25) issue of Rodale's New Shelter. Here an earth tube pioneer used eight 4-inch (10-centimeter) pipes laid in a flat trench under his home. (Figure 49) Each one is about 30 feet (9 meters) long. He reported that his earth tube (all eight pipes function as a single earth tube) were useful for "cooling" for only 15 minutes each day. Why so limited a useful time? The shortness of the tube is the major factor.

In the summer, power assisted convection sucks air into the home through the pipes, up through the home, and out through a fan at the top. Air entering the pipes is very warm, 85°F - 90°F (29°C - 32°C). Gradually the earth around the tube would heat up beginning near the outside opening. Then this warming effect would advance along the tube until it would reach the interior. At this point, the air began to enter the home at a higher temperature than the owner liked so he would shut them down. Twenty-four hours later he could repeat the same thing.

The place along the tube where the temperature has risen to that of the outdoor air will ADVANCE or RECEDE depending upon what is happening to the whole system. This moving point along the tube that is the same as the outdoor temperature is called a "WAVE-FRONT." If this wave-front happens to be colder than the indoor temperature then it could be called a cold-front. If it is warmer, it could be called a warm-front.

When the wave-front reaches the full length of the earth tube, the air entering the home will be the same temperature as when it entered the tube outside. Earth tubes that are about 60 feet long or longer (depending on the exact circumstances) tend to be operable continuously. That is, the wave-front never makes it all the way to the end. Thus longer tubes shouldn't have to be shut down periodically in order to let them regain their original temperature. But exactly how far the wave-front will travel is controlled by many factors.

Tubes in the Warm Earth

The configuration of Figure 49 has four inches of insulation underneath the entire basement floor, and over the top of the pipes. Apparently, by insulating the floor, it was expected that the earth would always rob the heat away to maintain its natural deep-earth temperature. That's why they mistakenly call them "cool tubes." This clearly demonstrates how our perception of how things will work affects the way we design things. Chapters 1 and 2 correct our understanding of how heat flows in the earth, so this knowledge can correct our design process.

The central part of the floor would have its temperature dominated by the heat flow through the earth tubes and to a lesser extent by the slow movement of heat through the insulation—even if it is four inches thick. Remember that insulation does not stop heat, it merely slows it down.

The outer perimeter of the earth under the home has its temperature dominated by both the outdoor weather and the earth tubes because it has less than ten feet or so of conductive path through the earth to the exposed outdoor surface.

Since the designer wanted to "cool" the air, it is ONLY the OUTER PORTIONS of the tube/earth combination (they function together) that are actually operating as he wishes. The warm air entering on the outer end caused the wave-front to move up the tube until it reached the central portion. Here, the earth was already warm because of prior earth tube use, and because heat from the basement floor has climatized THAT earth to a new, higher temperature. Since little or no heat exchange would occur between the air and the already warm earth, the warm-front moves rapidly onward to the other side of the house where it again encounters a portion of the tube whose cooler temperature is dominated by the average annual air temperature out-of-doors. Therefore, only two relatively short sections of pipe are actually doing the job desired.

What can we learned from all this?

FIRST: If you plan to use earth tubes FOR COOLING ONLY, do not put them under insulation, under a house, because it functions like an insulation/watershed umbrella. Earth tubes used for cooling MUST be placed WHERE THE EARTH IS ALWAYS COOL and is likely to remain that way. In this case a better choice would have been the back yard.

SECOND: 30-foot (9-meter) earth tubes are too small for most installations. While mild climates do not require extra-long tubes because the temperature differences are easier to work with, 60-foot (18-meter) tubes would probably be a good choice; but 100 to 200 feet (30 to 60 meters) of tube would be better, especially in colder climates.

THIRD: Tubes which are too short, or in less than optimum configurations only work for a short time each day. This is a symptom of basic design difficulties.

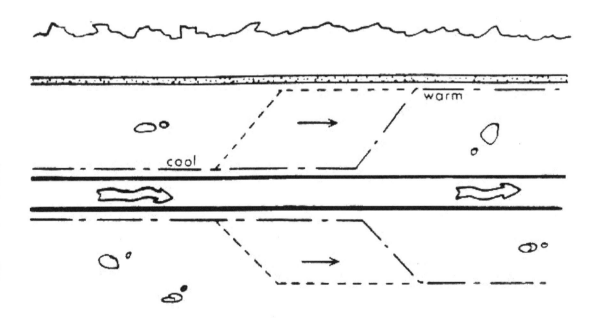

Figure 50 The advancing wintertime cold wave-front as the earth around the tube is progressively cooled off. If this wave-front reaches the interior, air will enter the home at the same temperature as it is outside.

through the pipe. When the pipe is shut down, and no air is moving, conduction in the earth will slowly soak up the newly inserted heat as it now becomes a part of the thermal earth-environment. That is, it gets muddled in with all of the other heat that's flowing around, following all the rules laid out in the first three chapters of this book.

FIFTH: A cold-front will advance and recede in just the same way as will a warm-front.

SIXTH: If the wave-front will advance by blowing air into the house it can also be made to recede by blowing air the other way. If we can make the tube "breathe," then the air will take turns going one way and then the other. In this way the wave-front can be kept from reaching the interior and bringing the outdoor weather directly inside. Thus the earth tube becomes a counterflow heat exchanger just like a camel's nose! However, we do not want to use this as an excuse for shortening the pipes since the breaths are not all the same length. Air may still flow in a single direction for quite a while before it reverses, although it will probably balance-out over the entire year.

SEVENTH: A much closer look should be given to the action of multiple pipes and how they relate to each other.

Earth Tubes that Breathe

How does each "breath" effect earth tube operation? What happens during each one? How does the tube length affect it? Let's examine the wintertime case where we wish to heat up incoming air. Then we can apply the principle to outgoing air, and summertime operation.

As cold air is being drawn through the tube, the earth gives up its heat to warm the air. That portion of the tube and earth which is nearest the cold outdoor opening will cool off first. To warm that air, heat must be conducted from elsewhere in the earth, naturally, that takes time. The warmer that earth is, the more heat is available for transferring to the interior of the home. Therefore, containing the heat with an umbrella will greatly enhance the earth tube operation.

Note the small insulation umbrella of Figure 57. This is included to give some thermal isolation to the pipe whenever it protrudes from under the main umbrella, but hasn't yet reached the open air. The earth temperature under it will be generally lower and therefore a smaller, thinner umbrella, 8 feet wide by 1 inch thick minimum, (3 meters wide by 3 centimeters thick) should allow that earth near the tube to have its temperature controlled by the temperature inside the pipe rather than from the earth's surface.

As the outer end of the tube is cooled by the inhaling breath, the air takes its needed heat from a place farther up the pipe, towards the house. This "cold-front" gradually moves up the pipe. If this cold wave-front reaches the inside, as with shorter tubes, the air will come into the house cold. With long tubes, the heat has more opportunity to migrate from the deeper earth, up to the pipe. When conduction replaces the heat, it retards the advancing cold-front. If it can replace the heat fast enough then the cold-front will be pushed back toward the outside opening. In arctic climates, the cold-front advances more rapidly because of the very low air temperatures. Therefore, very long tubes would be needed.

Since it is actual heat that must be replaced BTU for BTU, the speed of the advancing cold-front can be regulated by controlling the amount of heat taken out. Hence, a tube which has a high powered fan will sap off the available heat much faster than slower ones, or convection operated ones.

Breathing occurs when the air flow is periodically reversed. Now the heat from the house is saved for return on the next breath by the 'camel's nose' effect. That is, the heat from inside warms up the earth around the tube during this "exhaling" breath, which had been cooled by the prior "inhaling" breath. Like the previous breath, this one may actually take many hours, during which, the cold-front is pushed backwards down the pipe. If this breath were long enough, the earth would all heat up to room temperature. Then the cold-front would be pushed all the way out, dumping valuable energy into the cold winter air.

Therefore, if you were to measure the air temperature a few feet up inside each end of the earth tube, you could determine how well it is working. If air is flowing and the indoor temperature is nearly the same as the air coming into the home, (measured from the inside of the pipe,) then they are functioning just like you want them to. The further they are from this ideal, the less efficient they are. Or to look at it another way, the tubes are designed to maintain a temperature differential from one end to the other. The closer this is to the temperature difference between indoors and outdoors the more efficient they are, if air is flowing. (Assuming the inside is at the temperature you desire.) If they work this way continually, then you have achieved all the goals earth tubes are meant to.

How Earth Tube Operation
Is Affected by the Diameter

Most earth tubes are from 4 inches to 18 inches (10 to 45 centimeters) in diameter. Four inch tubes are generally chosen over 8-inch ones because they are cheaper. But smaller pipes are harder to get air through.

The ease with which air can be pushed through a pipe depends on the square area of pipe cross section, and its length. The formula for calculating the area of cross section of a round pipe is:

$A = 3.14 R^2$

A = area of cross section

R = radius of the pipe (half the diameter)

Note what happens when you use a bigger pipe. If the radius, and thus the diameter, is doubled then the area is quadrupled. That is, an 8-inch (20-centimeter) pipe has four times as much area as a 4-inch (10-centimeter) pipe. But two 4-inch (10-centimeter) pipes have only twice the area. Which means, if you use 4-inch (10-centimeter) pipe to produce the same cross section as a single 8-inch (20-centimeter) pipe, then you must use FOUR of them.

Why would you want to use four pipes in place of one? Because of an economic paradox. 4-inch (10-centimeter) pipe is more popular than 8-inch (20-centimeter). Since people buy more of it, its price is much lower than the 8-inch. In fact, it is often cheaper to buy four feet of 4-inch than a single foot of 8-inch. This is especially true if you select garden variety (or should I say, "sewer variety") PVC pipe—DRAIN TILE!

Ah ha! Someone will say, "I can get volume prices, and maybe even use my drain tile around the home as an earth tube!" Yes, but BE CAREFUL! Drain tile has water removal as its main purpose, but an earth tube's is AIR transport. These two functions can interfere with one another. So read carefully the sections that follow on humidity and moisture in the tubes before you attempt to combine functions. But you can use the same type of pipe, and still get your volume discount.

Along with the lower price of using four smaller pipes rather than using a single 8-inch one, we get a bonus: TWICE the thermal connection to the earth and greater versatility. The thermal connection (that is, its ability to move heat into and out of the earth,) is determined by the SURFACE AREA OF THE PIPE. The pipe's surface is equal to the circumference times the length.

The thermal connection between a pipe and the earth is determined by the R-value of the plastic, (or whatever the pipe is made of,) its thickness, and its size (surface area). Drain tile is so thin that the "R" becomes less important than the need for permanence and water tightness that you get with plastic rather than metal. Since the R-value has become less important than the surface area, let's compare the surfaces of various sizes of pipes so we can get an idea of the choices we have.

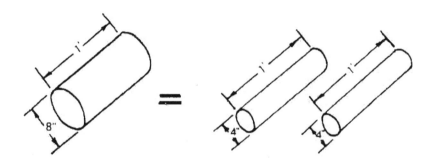

As we compare the use of single pipes to multiple pipes, let's not confuse using multiple pipes with the basic requirement of having TWO earth tubes for each house: an inlet AND an outlet. Both are required. So, when I am discussing multiple pipes, I mean using more than one pipe to REPLACE one or both of the earth tubes. TOGETHER THE MULTIPLE PIPES FUNCTION AS ONE EARTH TUBE.

Now for a simple comparison to see what happens when we go from a single pipe to multiple pipes. Look closely at the following table.

Number of Pipes	Diameter	Cross Section Area	Surface Area Per Foot of Pipe
1	8	50.3	301.6
4	4	50.3	603.2
3	4	37.7	452.4
2	4	25.1	301.6
1	4	12.6	150.8

Notice that some have the same cross section, some have two times as much and some four times. This comparison is here to give you an idea of what each choice will do.

Each of these sizes should work well, but each has its own attributes, and each has its own applications. There are, as yet, no standards: only suggestions. Big buildings, with lots of people in them, need more air, and thus a greater total cross-section. Small homes with small needs require something else. Our goal is to give you the tools to work with.

Most of the earth tubes that have been reported on in the popular media have been designed to work with fans. Those which do use convection are generally much larger. A smaller opening area will be harder to force air through, too small an area could prevent convective flow altogether. However, the reason for choosing very large pipes may not be as valid as is often supposed.

The sizes are usually chosen by using the air flow formulae for forced air ducting (pipes that have fans on them). There is some indication that the slow moving convective currents do not encounter the same resistance to air flow as would be encountered by the swiftly moving forced air. Therefore, convection may work quite well using pipes that are much smaller than most people suspect. However, I cannot give you an exact size! This is still a pioneering work, and as yet no optimum sizes have been agreed upon. This is also true because there are a multitude of other factors which play an important role in designing earth tubes. That's what makes this work so much fun!

Multiple and Single Pipes

The use of multiple pipes provides us with some interesting new design possibilities. First of all, let's examine how the use of multiple pipes will affect their length. Multiple pipes are used to REPLACE ONE OR BOTH of the earth tubes, (upper or lower). The effects are similar on each, so we need examine only the case where multiple pipes are used to replace ONE of the earth tubes.

Eight pipes were used in the above example from the innovative pioneer reported on in New Shelter magazine, to replace a single earth tube. The group of pipes function as a single tube since air ENTERS the home through them all at the same time. No doubt, the cost of a single pipe, and the additional pipe surface were the major reasons why one would want to choose a method such as this. Increasing the surface of the pipe is good, because you get a better thermal connection to the soil. However, do not expect that this extra surface will make up for a drastic reduction in the length of the entire tube.

The over-all length of the tube is decided upon by the characteristics of the EARTH itself. This is true whether single or multiple pipes are used. Being a fairly good conductor, the earth will SHORT OUT portions of the tube that are near each other just like it did around the end of the insulation umbrella in Chapter 2. Therefore, the change in earth temperature from one foot to the next, along each pipe, will always be small. This effect can be compared to the heat flow through a simple conductive Isolation Zone as described in Chapters 1 & 2.

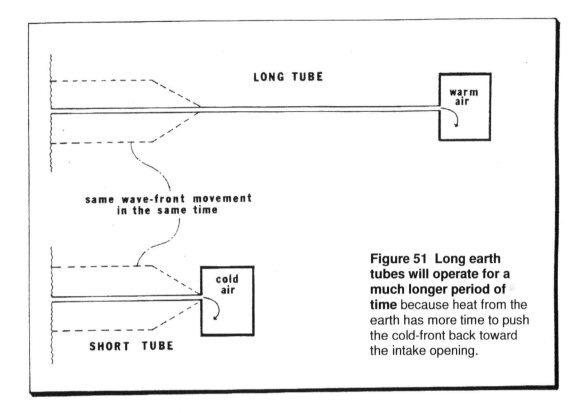

LONG TUBE

warm
air

same wave-front movement
in the same time

cold
air

SHORT TUBE

Figure 51 Long earth tubes will operate for a much longer period of time because heat from the earth has more time to push the cold-front back toward the intake opening.

The temperature difference from one side of an Isolation Zone to the other may, at times, be over 100°F (56°C) in some installations. That amount is spread over 7 to 10 feet (2 to 3 meters) of temperature moderating earth. The earth tube must also spread this temperature difference from its outer end to its inner end. The earth tube though, is actually bringing the surface weather deep within its "Isolation Zone." Thus the wave-front of cold winter or hot summer temperatures will move into the earth much more rapidly. A much longer distance, 60 or more feet (18 meters), will be required to effectively isolate the interior temperatures from winter's storms, and summer's hot spells, than would be required with a simple conductive Isolation Zone. Therefore, more, but shorter, pipes WILL NOT DO!

While the use of multiple pipes does not give us reason to shorten the over-all earth tube, the pipe layout does give us some interesting design possibilities because of the way that near-by pipes will affect each other.

Parallel Pipes

Each earth tube may be made of several pipes. For a given total cross section of pipe, multiple pipes have a better thermal connection with the ground, but only if they are installed correctly. Conduction through the earth between pipes or even between two parts of the same pipe, determines how different pipe configurations will work.

Figure 52 shows several possible layouts. In the arrangement in Figures 52-A & B the pipes interfere with each other, because the earth between them will short them out by quickly coming to the temperature in the tube. This causes them to act as if they were a single pipe trying to move heat into or out of the greater body of earth. Therefore, the additional pipe surface has been rendered completely ineffective.

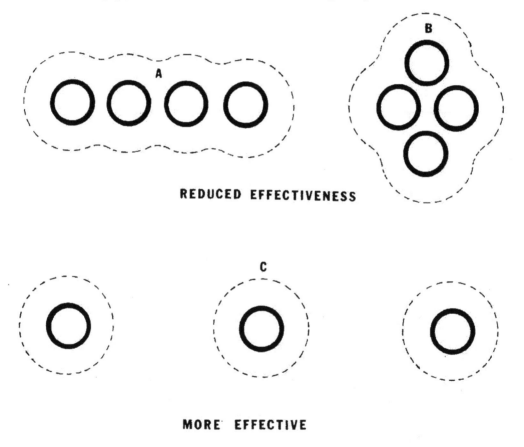

Figure 52 Several possible layouts for using (parallel flowing) pipes to replace one of the earth tubes. A and B interfere with one another and function like a single pipe with a smaller surface area. C will operate much longer before interference occurs.

To avoid a direct thermal connection between the pipes, they should be separated. Separating them is a better idea IF the air in them is moving in the SAME direction, and you are not trying to build a counterflow heat exchanger. (Figure 52-C) But, how much should you separate them?

The exact amount of separation will vary from one home to another; from one locale to another; and from one end of the tube to the other. The earth is quite forgiving, so we do not need to calculate the optimum distance to the millimeter. We do, however, need to know approximately what the effect will be.

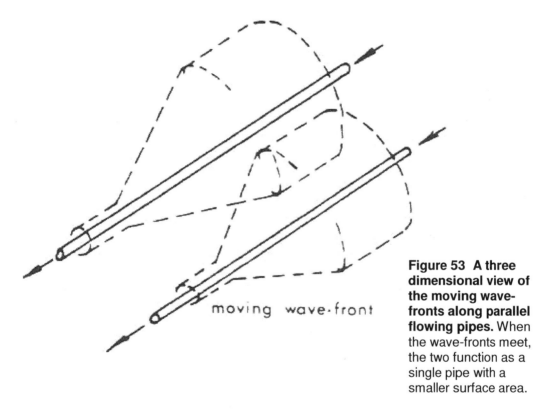

moving wave·front

Figure 53 A three dimensional view of the moving wave-fronts along parallel flowing pipes. When the wave-fronts meet, the two function as a single pipe with a smaller surface area.

If we choose 4 feet (1.2 meters) as an example of a separating distance, notice, that the wave-front will soak into the ground with the same speed as it does in the Moderation Zone on top of an earth sheltered home, but with one major difference. The outdoor temperatures are advancing into the earth from both pipes. This sideways-moving wave-front is headed into the earth in between the pipes, from both sides. (Figure 53) Therefore, it will function as if it were only ONE HALF as thick as a Moderation Zone. A 4-foot (1.2-meter) thick separation will moderate-out about ONE DAY'S worth of temperature fluctuations.

In many installations, a 4-foot (1.2-meter) separation will be quite sufficient, but in more severe climates the separation should be even greater. After all, when the wave-fronts meet, the two pipes again function as one, and the effectiveness of their heat exchange will be reduced. Also, close pipes make the wave-front moving along them go faster.

However, you will probably not be able to tell the difference when this occurs, unless your tubes are unusually short. When the effectiveness of the pipes is reduced for any reason, the amount of time they may be used before the outdoor temperatures enter directly into the home will be likewise reduced.

Therefore, by separating the pipes, their entire surface will become an effective heat exchanger, and we may gain the advantages of using multiple pipes to replace one or both of the earth tubes.

Tubes Near the Surface or Near the Home

It can be easily seen from this discussion, the importance of having all the earth tubes UNDERNEATH an insulation umbrella. If they were not, then the outdoor temperatures would enter from the exposed surface spoiling the temperature environment we are trying to create with the tubes. In the winter for example, the umbrella will contain the heat that had been stored last summer. The more heat there is available, the longer the tubes can function. The cold wave-front which moves up each tube towards the house would be very slow in warm earth. And as the tubes breathe, they will replace that heat with heat from the interior, and conduction will replace it from the surrounding earth. If the tubes were near the outdoor surface, without an umbrella, the earth about them would cool off from above, and valuable heat would be lost to the open air.

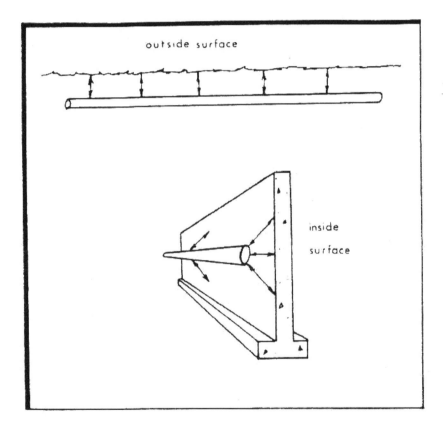

Figure 54 Tubes near an exposed surface, inside or out, will have the earth temperature around them dominated by the air temperature at the larger surface. If the outside is cold, the earth tubes will produce cold air. If the outside is warm, they will produce warm air. That's why they should be put under an umbrella; you can control their operational temperature.

Likewise, the earth's shorting-out effect is more pronounced NEAR the home itself than it is deeper into the dirt. Since the walls, floor, and maybe the roof of the home also conduct heat to and from the heat-saving earth, the tubes should not be put in close proximity to them either. Tubes that must travel along walls, under floors and the like, should be kept 8 to 10 feet (2.4 to 3 meters) away from the building, where possible.

Earth Tube Layout

Earth tubes are going to be a major component of the home's site plan. They take up a lot of space, and require a lot of planning. Since they are so long, we will naturally try to squeeze them into much smaller spaces to make room for a myriad of other things we would like to fit onto our lot. I'm sure someone will even try to cram 200 feet (60 meters) of earth tube under a 20-foot (6-meter) umbrella!

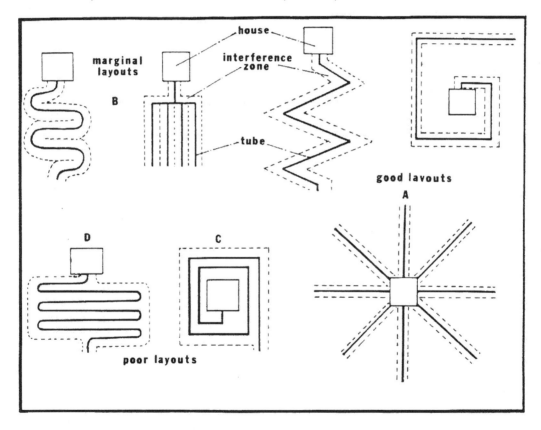

Figure 55 Various arrangements for single and multiple pipes. Each constitutes a single earth tube even though they may muse many parallel flowing pipes.

Take a look at Figure 55. The dotted lines show a 2-foot (0.6-meter) zone which goes all the way around each pipe. This could be called an "interference zone." Within this distance the interference zone of another pipe, or a conductive surface, would affect that pipe within twenty-four hours. This problem occurs whether you are using a single pipe as an earth tube, or multiple pipes, since it will occur between separate pipes as well as nearby parts of the same pipe.

Figure 55 A and B show only one of the two required earth tubes laid out so that interference would be minimal. These are by no means the only arrangements. They simply show how the idea of an interference zone can be applied.

Figure 55 C and D have a problem. Their parts do not get further apart from each other as the temperature differential in the pipe gets larger. A 4-foot separation will be insufficient when the temperature difference between one pipe and another becomes large. This temperature difference, along with the expected time delay through the earth, determines how much interference will occur. THEY ARE TOO CLOSE TOGETHER!

Large portions of each pipe are shorted out by the conductive earth. If you must lay your earth tubes in a configuration similar to Figure 55 D, you should keep the sections very small, as in B. The smaller sections do not have the high temperature difference, and therefore, a smaller amount of earth separation will suffice.

The other earth tube (single or multiple-pipe set) will affect the first earth tube (single or multiple-pipe set) differently, because the air is moving in the OPPOSITE direction.

Counterflow Layouts

What if the air in the tubes is going in OPPOSITE directions? That is, one tube brings air into the home, and the other takes it out. In this case you must determine from your over-all goals, whether you wish to have a counterflow heat exchange in addition to that of the "camel's nose" effect. That is, actual heat exchange from the air in one tube to the air in the other. If you desire such a heat transfer, then the tubes SHOULD BE PLACED RIGHT NEXT TO EACH OTHER. If you DO NOT WANT this effect then they should be separated. In order to use the counterflow principle, BOTH EARTH TUBES MUST BE USED. Counterflow heat exchange between different parts of a single tube would be self-defeating, just as with the shorting-out effect explained above.

A counterflow heat exchanger will isolate the outdoor weather from the indoor temperatures. They are designed to maintain a temperature difference across them, keeping it warm inside and cold outside (in the winter) for example.

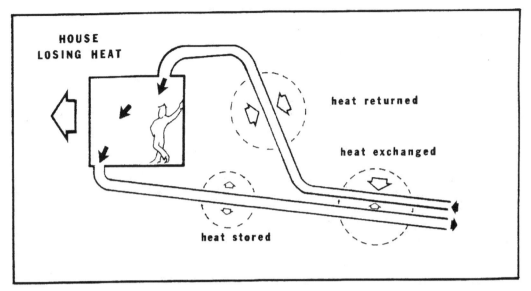

Figure 56 side by side earth tubes used as a counterflow heat exchanger.

In the basic, convection-operated earth tube arrangement discussed at the beginning of this chapter, (Figure 46) a counterflow heat exchanger would work well, and would save on the number of trenches that must be dug. The LOWER portion of the UPPER tube, and ALL of the LOWER tube could be laid in the earth side by side. If multiple pipes are used for either or both of the tubes, then they should be laid alternately, an input, and an output-input, output and so on, so pipes that are a part of the same tube are NOT adjacent to each other. (Figure 56)

This general layout (Figure 46) uses the home as a passive solar collector. If your design does not use the home in this way, a counterflow heat exchange arrangement may not be the best way to go. (Chapters 9 and 10 examine some of the other uses that earth tubes can perform, such as adjusting the earth's constant temperature and retrofitting pre-existing homes.) If your design uses the warm summer AIR as the MAIN source of heat, then the earth environment will require its heat to be replenished through the tubes only. Or if your design needs to RE-establish a comfortable temperature in the storage zone more often than just at the initial time right after construction, as with earth sheltered homes, then counterflow earth tubes (because of design limitations, in these cases,) should not be used.

An example of this is when the warm summer air is drawn through BOTH EARTH TUBES at the same time, by using the home as a solar chimney (dumping heat out the roof, to cause the earth tubes to function convectively. When both tubes are thus used, they really function as if they were a double set of pipes of a single earth tube, since the air is going in the SAME direction, into the home. This allows the deep-earth temperature to be adjusted, whereas the normal operation tends to maintain the status quo.

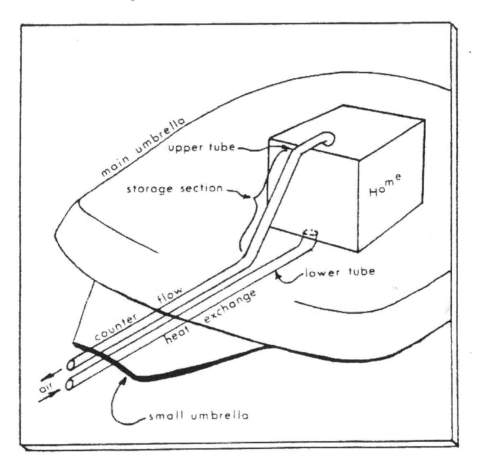

Figure 57 Layering the lower parts of both earth tubes side by side in the same trench makes them function as a counterflow heat exchanger. The earth conducts heat between them in addition to the "camel's nose" effect.

All of this may seem more complex than is usually necessary, but what other book tells you how to do it, if you wish to use these features?

Earth tubes really are versatile. There are many things we can do with them, such as the convectively powered earth tube pair in Figure 46. Convective powered earth tubes have two other important criteria.

Altitude and Temperature Difference

A chimney works because there is a temperature difference from one end to the other; the smoke is contained, and allowed to rise. It is convectively powered. The greater the temperature difference, the hotter the fire, and/or the taller the chimney, the faster the smoke goes out. Homes, earth tubes and other things can work the same way, although their temperature differences are smaller.

If a house is warm inside, and it has a hole in the ceiling and a hole in the wall next to the floor, then convection will cause the heat to be dumped out the top. If such an arrangement is intentional, and uses the sun's power to make it happen, it is CALLED a "solar chimney."

Earth tubes can also function like a chimney. The basic requirements are:

1. A pipe or tube open on both ends.
2. An altitude difference from one end of the tube to the other. (One end is high, and the other low.)
3. A source of heat that can cause a temperature difference from one end to the other.

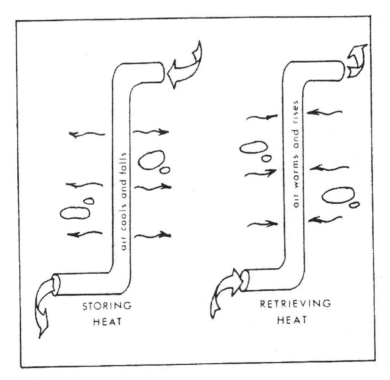

Figure 58 The temperature and altitude difference in a convectively operated tube or chimney determines how much air will be moved through the tube regardless of whether it is being cooled or heated by the earth around it.

138

The stored heat, or the heat being stored, depending on which way the air is moving, supplies the power to make the convectional earth tubes work. The actual temperatures depend on many things; the whole range of this book's subject matter. The altitude difference, though, is something YOU DESIGN.

Since earth tubes should have differences in their levels from one end to the other, flat or only slightly sloping tubes will not cause convection. They will require fans or other means of forcing the air to go where it won't go naturally. Of course this may present some siting problems since it is difficult enough to gain 8 or 10 feet (2.4 or 3 meters) of rise in the upper earth tube even if your house is on a hill, without trying to do it on flat ground. If your lot is flat, the tubes can open into an excavation for a driveway, or whatever, and then they should work well. However, the excavation must be large enough to allow a free flow of air. And adjacent earth tube openings should be arranged so that one doesn't suck in the stale air exhausted by the other.

Earth tubes connected as in Figure 46, DO NOT operate on the temperature difference between the inside and the outside of the home. They work because of the difference in temperature between the HOME and the earthen STORAGE ZONE. That is why the outer openings of the tubes exit the earth AT THE SAME LEVEL. (This is difficult to show on flat drawings.)

But even the lower earth tube must have a slope. It functions like the thermal syphon, which is a heat trap. Figure 59 Chillie Willie's NEW igloo is a heat trap.

Chilly Willy and the Heat Trap

This is Chilly Willy's[1] igloo!

Chilly Willy is cold all the time because his igloo has not been designed like REAL igloos and snow shelters up north. Figure 59 is how it is really done.

Here the home functions as a HEAT TRAP. The small narrow opening limits the amount of wind that can blow in. The altitude difference confines the warm air up in the home, while cooler air will descend into the entryway as it is a "cold sump." If there is no altitude difference, then the cold air will just wash in and out of its own free will. In fact the difference in level must be greater than the height of the door. Earth tubes and entries (even those with two doors, air locks, or foyers) should always be made this way in very cold climates, and would work well in more moderate climates too.

> Chilly Willy had a door,
> It made him make his fire roar.
> Because his home was built so silly,
> That's why they call him "Chilly Willy."
>
> Now he's changed his entryway,
> To save the heat he gains each day.
> It took some thought for Chilly Willy,
> But now he won't be chilly, will he!

---

[1] Chilly Willy is a copyrighted cartoon character owned by Lantz/Universal.

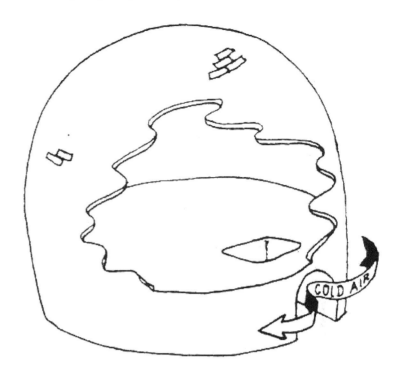

Figure 59 Chilly Willy's new igloo is a heat trap.

Like Chilly Willy's door, earth tubes should always have an altitude difference, because they too must function as heat traps.

Water and Air... Controlling Humidity

The amount of water which is in the air is measured as "relative humidity." Our comfort is influenced not so much by the quantity of water, but by the amount of water present for a given temperature. Warm air will hold considerably more water than cool air. Air which has a given amount of water vapor in it may seem dry to us when it is warm, but the same amount of water in cool air will be wet. Since the temperature influences humidity and earth tubes affect the temperature, the relative humidity will be greatly affected when using earth tubes.

The factors we must work with are:

1. The outdoor air has a certain amount of water in it. This is what we must work with since it is set by our climate.
2. Our preferences since some people like it humid, others do not. Generally people complain if they are uncomfortable, but seldom do they praise an arrangement if the humidity is just right. So if no one gripes, your tubes are probably doing fine.

3. If the incoming air is to be cooled, then the air will be more humid. If we expected it to be too humid, we should take definite steps to dehumidify it.

4. If the incoming air is to be warmed, then the air will be dryer, and we may wish to humidify it.

5. So in the summer it may be wet and the winter it may be dry.

In the past, there seem to have been more complaints about wet air than dry air. Some earth tube systems will soak you to the skin, others work very well, even in the same climate. Let's determine why, so ours will work as we wish them to.

Humidity in Summer Air – Dehumidification

Only when mushrooms are in a salad are they and people comfortable at the same time. Mushrooms like it dark and damp. People like it sunlit and dry. An earth shelter designed as this book depicts would be warm, sunny, and DRY. Since we have already taken care of every source of water by controlling it, and directing it from where we get it to where we want it; the last remaining water source is the AIR ITSELF. This we are stuck with, unless we wish to move elsewhere.

If you live in a dry summer climate, a little extra moisture will be welcome. If you live in a wet climate the earth tubes will make it all the wetter, because condensation will take place in the pipe whenever moist air is being cooled. The usual way of handling excess moisture is to raise the temperature in the house, but that is the very thing we are trying to avoid in the first place.

If your climate is really wet, the air may still be too wet for comfort. In this case, you must install a dehumidifier or do without the benefits of fresh air; just as you must with ANY OTHER kind of ventilation system. We will briefly examine two possibilities for handling the water problems for those few places that may need extra dehumidification: the mechanical and the passive.

You may prefer to buy a dehumidifier that stands alone in the house, rather than attempting to connect it to the earth tubes. This is especially true if your earth tubes are arranged so that air must move both ways, into and out of, the tubes. This is an arrangement that would require extensive piping, one way valves and the like to connect the dehumidifier directly. However, in many climates most of the air entering the home in the summer will come through the lower earth tube, since in the summer more heat is being stored via the upper tube.

This imbalance may allow you to attach the dehumidifier to the lower tube, and catch most of the moist air. Another alternative would be to hang one on each of the tubes, (an idea that would work, but an expensive one). But in most cases where humidity is a problem a commercial dehumidifier is the best answer. At this time.

For the more imaginative reader, the real pioneer in underground heat flow, there is another idea that is at least fun to look at.

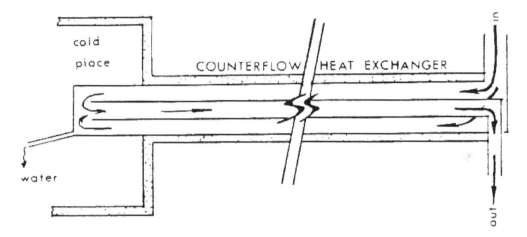

Figure 60 An experimental arrangement for dehumidifying moist air.

Figure 60 shows an unusual passive arrangement using a special counterflow heat exchanger that causes the air to cool off just enough to condense out the majority of the water. Then the air is returned to almost its original input temperature, and the resulting lower relative humidity.

You'll have to pay close attention to this one!

The original earth tube cooled the moist summer air just enough to make its TEMPERATURE comfortable. To dehumidify it, we must artificially drop its temperature a little more so that much more water will condense out and then return it to the comfortable temperature WITHOUT so much water. VOILA! DRY, COMFORTABLE AIR!

The dehumidifier is SEPARATE from the earth tubes and it would be connected just as with the commercial variety. The counterflow heat exchanger keeps the whole arrangement reasonably efficient and is insulated because it has a temperature difference from one end to the other that we do not want to be fouled up by heat conduction through the surrounding warm earth. The "cold place" is made cold artificially by whatever method you choose.

Here are some suggestions.
1. A refrigerator.
2. An ice house.
3. The outdoor deep-earth temperature, if your average annual air temperature is low enough, and this tube is plenty long enough to reach it outside of the warm earth environment you have artificially created around your home. That could be quite a distance.
4. A permanent cold storage place built using the passive annual heat storage methods as described in Chapter 10. (Now, that sure would be an exotic arrangement!)

Another Thought

You know, a camel's nose stores water as well as heat. If an arrangement could be made that would soak up moisture when the air is moving in one direction, and replace it when the air is moving in the other direction, and one such device were placed on each earth tube, then the home would maintain a moisture level at whatever you adjust it to. But alas, we will have to wait for some clever person to come up with one.

Humidity in Winter Air

Winter air is colder and has less moisture. Thus the problem may be dryness. One way HUMIDIFICATION may be done is by placing a commercial or homemade humidifier at the mouth of the tube which brings in the most air in the winter. Depending on your climate this tube will be the upper one, the one that brings in heat from storage. The exiting air is generally the big wintertime problem. Internal air is warm and often moisture laden. This condensate, may freeze if it is allowed to run all the way outside.

Therefore, it should be drained into the earth before it reaches a cold place in the earth tube.

Earth Tube Drainage

Drainage for both earth tubes is very important. This drainage system is very closely tied in with the over-all drainage principles laid out in chapter 4. A dry earth environment is much easier to work with. But what do you suppose would happen if the earth were NOT DRY, in addition to all the bad thermal problems?

Earth tubes are drained with a very simple method; they have holes in them! If the air in the tubes is dry, or is warming up so that it can hold more water, it will take up any available water. Water that is already in the earth can go through drain holes into a pipe just as easily as it can go the other way!

So, if you don't take care of the water table in the proper way, you'll drown the tubes. If you don't take care of the water that soaks in from above, then the earth around the tubes will be moist, and so will your air. Many earth tube arrangements have had such artificially induced moisture problems. The point is: Always use an insulation/watershed umbrella over your earth tubes, as it will eliminate most moisture problems.

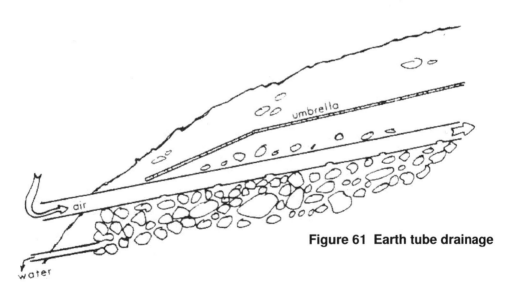

Figure 61 Earth tube drainage

The tube itself should be laid in a washed gravel bed so that moisture can drain away from the tube. If the soil around the tube has high clay content or has other natural drainage problems, then care should be taken to see that puddles will not form in the gravel just under it; the entire tube bed should be well drained. The whole length of the tube need not have drain holes in it, but it should have them far enough in from the outside, so that it will not freeze, probably at least half way in.

Also, drainage is especially difficult on flat land, since you must make provisions for handling all surplus water, and the gravel should be washed clean so that dust will not be drawn into the house.

The question then arises, "can the drain tile which is laid just below the footing, that is supposed to keep the backfill dry, be used as an earth tube?" Yes, if you are very careful. The two really have two different functions.

But it can, if the drain tile next to the home is only an emergency backup, and the soil has a good drainage arrangement.

After all, wouldn't an earth tube drain away any water that got into it anyway, since it must go downhill away from the home? In chapter 10, I is discussed the special uses of upside-down earth tubes, ones that slope toward the house. Such tubes require special drainage provisions up close to the home, and great care must be taken when designing them, especially in extreme climates, or when operating temperatures will be below freezing.

The Overall Result

What should be the over-all result? Let's review our main objectives in using earth tubes in the first place:

1. A continuous supply of fresh air is available all year around. Many mechanical systems are not used in the winter, and when they are used, they are designed to bring in a great body of air and then shut off. The continuous approach requires less machinery, less energy, and allows for the same air circulation without such large units as would ordinarily be used.

2. The air enters the home AT room temperature, so it is more comfortable.

3. The heat is stored in the earth for later use.

4. The heat is returned from the Storage Zone automatically, and without machinery or thermostats. It even works when the power is off.

5. The earth tubes can be easily extended out farther than that portion of the Storage Zone, which is accessible by conduction only. Therefore, the amount of accessible heat storage may be greatly increased.

6. A second heat flow path, other than only by conduction, has been added for moving heat into and out of storage.

7. The greater the temperature difference between the home and the earthen heat storage, thus the greater the need for heat or ventilation, the faster the air flows. If anything tries to suddenly raise or lower the temperature the earth tubes will work harder to try to even it out again.
8. The overall effect is to moderate out the temperature differences which occur, just as with conduction.
9. The earth tubes can be used to control the operational temperature of the house as outlined in Chapter 8.
10. This may prove to be the major method that could be used for adapting the principles outlined in this book for use with above-ground buildings and other heat storage needs, even retrofitting.

Details to Make them Work Better

Little creepy crawling things love to find all sorts of ways to come in for a visit. A good test is to have a picnic in your home and see how many ants show up. The outdoor opening to the earth tubes should be protected from a number of things, including bugs.

1. The tube should have a screen or other method of preventing unwanted entry.
2. Bushes of one sort or another are often put over the openings, this makes the entry air cooler in the summer, but also invites more bugs.
3. Condensation will occur inside the tube. Since bugs also like a little drink, they will be attracted by water. If the end is tilted down a little so the drainage is swift enough that the bugs don't have to go to the water, maybe they will tend to stay outside.
4. The tube should be situated so that it will not be covered by snow drifts, or ice jams.
5. Earth settling around the home can sheer off a pipe. Backfilling with gravel should prevent this if there is gravel stuffed tight under the tube.
6. If you choose to use fans, use reversible fans with a single fan on each tube and a manifold to the various rooms. Make them easily accessible and removable for cleaning. Or better yet, use a pipe for each fan.

Overcoming Convective Earth Tube Limitations

A tight house is NECESSARY for the system to work. If your house leaks or a window or door is open, the loop will stop because the resistance to air flow will be much less through the open window than through the earth tubes. So make them tight!

The basic passive configuration is powered by the temperature difference between the STORAGE ZONE and the HOME, NOT between indoor and outdoor temperatures. Although a number of interesting arrangements are possible using this latter method. When the temperature is the same inside as it is in the Storage Zone, NO AIR WILL FLOW. Providing earth tube openings at places where heat is naturally generated such as the kitchen will not only make it more enjoyable to be in the kitchen, but will power the fresh air system to boot. However, when the air is not flowing we can always MAKE IT flow.

Generally homes are fitted with a number of fans, that are exhausted through the roof, along with gobs of heat. Bathroom, kitchen, and Jenn-Air® fans are among those usually installed. These fans regularly dump tons of heat out of every house. In fact, because they are either continuously open or at best, poorly sealed, they usually waste heat EVEN WHEN THEY ARE TURNED OFF. It would be possible to connect these heat sources to the main earth tubes. However, the manifold arrangement, the required use of one way flapper valves, reversible fans, and other things necessary to keep bad smells from going from one room to the other really make it easier to use special earth tubes to store this heat, and then let conduction to bring it back.

While some may shudder to think of powering a beautifully simple, convective- operated earth tube system, it may be more prudent to utilize these many avenues of approach. After all, not all earth tube systems will have available all the facilities it takes to make a convective system work. Fans do have some definite advantages:

1. They are controllable (automatically, or manually).
2. They can be made reversible.
3. They are not too expensive to install or operate. A one sixth horsepower motor that runs one half of the time over a 31 day month, at 4.5 cents per KWH, costs only about $4.
4. They can power an earth tube system where passive systems are prevented from use by other factors.
5. They can be used to adjust the average temperature of the Storage Zone.

Some of the things that usually have vents that could be used with special earth tubes are:

- Bathrooms
- Kitchens
- Kitchen ranges
- Dryers
- Wood stoves, furnaces, fireplaces, Russian fireplaces (chimneys and combustion air inlets)
- Even attic vents for those who choose not to earth shelter the roof.

Some are easy to do, and others will take a little more thought.

A good example of this is the electric dryer which usually has its expensive heat vented directly outdoors. You could dump it indoors, but this often creates a humidity problem in addition to the problem of the lint that must be caught. The dryer is more often used when you DON'T need extra heat than when you do; logically, the heat should be saved for later use.

Venting appliances such as electric dryers through a special 4-inch (10-centimeter) tube would cure many problems. However, you should always provide a means of easy access for cleaning any earth tube that has lint, grease, or other things blowing into it. Sometimes filters should be used, and in other situations, just cleaning will do the trick.

You may wish to add a special earth tube for each of the usual fans that most homes have, and allow them to extract and store valuable BTU's. Then the main earth tubes and conduction will return that heat when needed. Using these fans with earth tubes can increase the over-all efficiency of our homes, and they allow us to tap into heat sources that would be wasted otherwise.

Radon & Formaldehyde –
Earth Tubes Go to Work

One difficulty that has been encountered with the tighter, energy efficient homes, is the accumulation of various gases. In the past, all the holes and cracks that were built in to a home allowed these gases and a great body of heat to blow away in the wind. The problem has been there all along for what used to be called a "well-built house," only it was referred to as "stuffy." When a room got stuffy, someone would open a window. But with the rising cost of energy, no one wants to open anything.

Nowadays we've found out what some of those gases were that were making homes uncomfortable and even unhealthy. One of the most important is formaldehyde. I suspect that there are a number of other harmful things that accumulate in homes that await identification. Formaldehyde is given off by more than just the urea-formaldehyde insulation that was popular years back. It is used in all sorts of products, especially ones that are glued together. In heavy quantities, and probably in small quantities over a long period of time, it tends to make people sick. The "ounce of prevention" is to simply bring in fresh air. Unfortunately, in many places the OUTSIDE air makes people sick too.

Radon is an inert gas that is given off by the natural breakdown of radium. Radon will not make a house stuffy. Like argon, neon, and helium; you cannot smell, feel, taste or see radon. If it weren't radioactive, you wouldn't care if a little of it seeped into your home.

Radioactivity is not to be taken lightly. However, all you have to do is say "RADIOACTIVE" and it scares the living daylights out of people, so, no doubt much of the publicity comes from those who would profit by keeping people away from energy saving home designs. But, if you ignores a problem, it won't go away. We can profit by becoming aware of the problem, and curing it where it exists. Recognize and identify it, and then design to reduce or eliminate it.

How big of a problem is radon gas? In most cases, the earlier underground home owners had no problem, or were aware of none. Whether or not a home may have a radon problem depends, first of all, on its intended location. Where proper ventilation is provided, the problem is easily taken care of, because it is one of slow accumulation, and as long as the outside air is ok, you've got it made.

Radium, and its daughter, radon are generally found deep within the earth. Radium is a solid, and therefore usually stays put. Radon is a gas, and given an opportunity to escape through any available crack, it will. Cracks made by people (mines, oil wells and the like) tend to go deep into the earth, allowing the release of the gas in much greater quantities than would ever occur naturally. Since radium is often present where other valuable minerals are located, mines and radon gas often go together. Some mining towns have such a large amount escaping into the air that it has become a noticeable health hazard ABOVE GROUND. Since radioactive substances have been shown to cause cancer, and some of the smelters which often accompany mining towns have gone belly-up, residents have rightly become aware of this pollution problem that has remained long after the other pollution problems went away.

If you plan to live in such a place then you should be seriously concerned. But staying awake all night will not help identify or cure it. The ONLY way to find out if radioactive anything may present a problem at your building site is with a Geiger counter.

Actual radiation that is given off by anything is quickly absorbed by the earth and/or concrete which surround it. Only gamma rays will make it even a few feet before they are absorbed. If any radioactive substance is close enough to the surface to cause a problem, it may be detected before the excavation is made, but not necessarily.

When you make the excavation itself, a check with the Geiger counter will probably only tell you if SOLID radioactive substances are present in the hole, since the radon will be blown away in the wind. It would be better to check your neighbors' basements, especially if these have been closed up for a number of months and see if there is a noticeable difference between the amount of "background radiation" that is detected outside, you always have some and that collected in the basement.

Sometimes a radon scare story will be quick to remind us that radon gas is given off by the concrete from which we make our under-ground houses. As if it weren't given off by the concrete used to build high-rise office buildings.

However, knowledge is the first line of defense. If there is NO radium in the concrete it will NOT produce any radon gas. Radium is not to my knowledge, a regular additive for concrete. But, if the cement plant has radium in its gravel, you will have radium and radon its by-product, in your home. If a Geiger counter goes bananas at the ready-mix plant don't even use it on the driveway! One should be especially cautious if the ready-mix plant uses mine tailings to make its gravel. But generally this is not a problem. Most places do not have such high concentrations of radioactive materials.

The most common problem is the ACCUMULATION of radon, formaldehyde, Aunt Lizzie's bad cooking smell and Uncle Harry's cigar smoke. Ventilation is the cure. Continuous ventilation would be even better. What can provide this better than earth tubes?

Carbon Monoxide – The Silent Killer

One of the not-so-publicized problems is the accumulation of carbon monoxide (CO). Carbon monoxide is odorless, tasteless, invisible and deadly. It is the product of incomplete combustion. In the home it is usually produced by gas appliances of various kinds. Properly designed and installed appliances usually eliminate the CO up the chimney, which is all well and good. But, a crumby crumbly chimney can also allow it in from a wood stove, especially an airtight one. The major problem, however, is the interaction between appliances.

Fireplaces and wood stoves, because of their high temperatures, have a strong draw. That is, they act like big pumps that suck tons of air out of the house. That air must come from somewhere. If the house is tight, and has few cracks to let the air in, the fireplace will draw air from any available opening.

Gas appliances are purposely built with a hole in the chimney! The hole, which is covered with a funnel shaped piece of metal, keeps the pilot light from being blown out by the wind. The funnel also hides the hole so that most people don't see it. So, what happens when the wood stove sucks air and the gas appliance is the ONLY available inlet? The stove will draw air backwards down the gas flue, through the house, and into the stove. The gas appliance, and even its pilot light, is a very efficient manufacturer of carbon monoxide. When it is kept in the flue it's ok. But when another appliance sucks it into the living quarters, it is DEADLY.

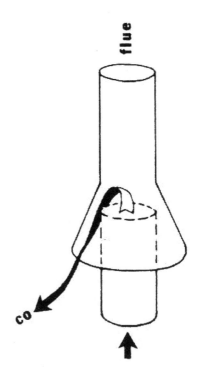

LOW PRESSURE

inside home

Figure 62 Funnel-shaped gas flue allows carbon monoxide to be sucked backwards into a tight house.

To counteract this problem, a pipe that brings in combustion air to the stove is usually required by the building code. This measure certainly has saved a lot of lives, since the stove will suck air from this pipe rather than the gas appliance. In an earth sheltered home that pipe is of necessity an earth tube. Therefore, air which enters the stove is warm air. Since this air is exhausted up the chimney, it could just as easily be stale air from inside that is replaced by fresh air from the earth tubes. However, it may be best not to have gas appliances at all with such an arrangement.

Earth Tubes to the Rescue

As complex as the previous discussion is, the cure for all of these problems is very simple: FRESH AIR. Earth tubes will give us a continuous supply of fresh air; fresh air for people, fresh air for combustion, fresh air for plants, fresh air without the usual heat loss, fresh air AT ROOM TEMPERATURE. And as the old song goes: "Who could ask for anything more?"

Notes:

Chapter 8 – Hot & Cold Running Radiant

Solar energy passes through the lens of an old timer's magnifying glass, to kindle a campfire while the youngsters stare on in amazement. First, a spot so bright you can't quite look at it appears on the shavings. Then a curling wisp of smoke, red glowing spots surrounded by blackened rings, and dancing purple spots that hang in your eyes, even when you look away. Then as quick as a kernel of popcorn jumps out of a popper, the yellow-orange flame bursts onto the scene with the crackle of a friendly fire, the shouts and laughter of hungry kids, and the smile of a wise old man.

Solar energy, focused through inquisitive minds of young and old alike, set in a scene of dwindling fossil fuels and skyrocketing power bills has kindled its radiant flame in the imaginations of back yard innovators and high-rise professionals. As curious children are dazzled by fire from a lens, so the lure of putting solar energy to work has intrigued the wise, and those who hope to become wise.

The primary energy source for Passive Annual Heat Storage is the sun. The heat which is to be stored is originally solar heat. The old timer's magnifying glass is a tool for using sunlight to accomplish a certain job: starting a fire. The earth sheltered home is a solar collector; a tool for collecting heat at a lower temperature, one which is just a little warmer than ordinary room temperature.

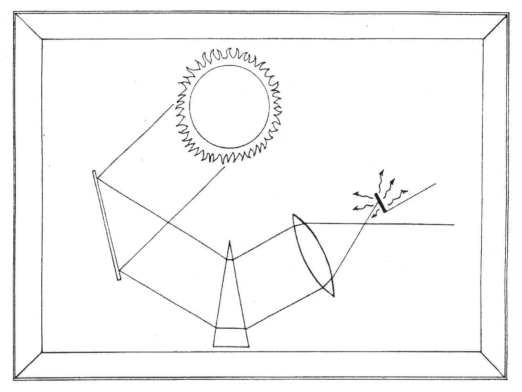

Figure 63 Radiant heat travels in a straight line. It may be reflected, refracted, focused, absorbed, re-radiated at a different wavelength, and is not affected by gravity.

Radiant Heat Flow

Radiant heat is familiar to all of us. Good old sunshine. Wood stoves too produce radiant heat. This radiant heat, also called infrared light, has some fine qualities that are not as often used as they could be.

Radiant heat travels in a straight line, and is not affected by gravity. It does not rise when it is warm as with convection. If sunlight enters a home at a lower elevation than the main body of the house, it's easier to use convection to move it to the upper portions of the home. It's much harder if it comes in upstairs, for then it must be pumped downstairs. Therefore, radiant heat transfer is a fine way to move heat DOWN.

Radiant heat may be reflected by a mirror or a piece of aluminum foil, refracted and focused as in the old timer's reading glass, absorbed or re-radiated. These are a whole new set of tools that are unavailable with other heat flow methods.

Heat and Temperature

There is an important difference between heat and temperature that can be illustrated with a magnifying glass. The amount of solar HEAT going through a magnifying glass and a piece of flat glass the same size will be the same. The sunlight that goes through the plane glass feels WARM; the focal point behind the magnifier is HOT. A lens capable of starting a campfire could even be made out of ice, because the temperature of the unconcentrated heat is low. The same amount of heat concentrated on to a tiny area raises the TEMPERATURE much more, but the actual amount of HEAT, the actual number of calories, is the same.

A calorie is the small amount of HEAT it takes to raise one cubic centimeter (one gram) of water 1E Celsius. Two calories will raise that same water 2E. But 2 calories of heat put into 4 cc of water will raise its temperature only one half of a degree.

The type of calorie used in measuring food value (actually a kilocalorie, kcal) is a thousand times bigger than the calorie usually used when talking about heat flow.

There are 251.99 calories in a single BTU.

A BTU (British Thermal Unit) is the amount of heat it takes to raise 1 pound of water 1° Fahrenheit. 2 BTU will raise that pound of water 2° or 4 lb. of water half of a degree.

Unfortunately, many people have made broad generalities about how radiant heat flow works, and have constructed things that could really be improved with a closer look at the way radiant heat flows and is used. I will touch only briefly on some of these as they apply to solar heated homes.

Hot-Shot Heating

Sunshine is usually measured in BTUs per HOUR. Therefore the more hours that the solar energy is available, the more heat will be collected. One of the reasons we have winter is because the days are shorter and therefore, fewer BTUs are available to keep us warm.

A large amount of sunlight coming all at once through a big south-facing window may provide the same amount of heat (BTUs or calories) as three smaller windows (one each on the east, west and south,) but because the heat collection with the 3 smaller ones will be spread out over a longer time period, the temperatures will be more moderate.

If overheating occurs, it may not be because there is an excess of heat, so much as, an excess of temperature because the home was unable to store the heat fast enough. Overheating can occur when using the "hot-shot" method of solar collection, (large windows facing in one direction only) because the thermal mass in the building responds much better if the heat input covers a longer time-span (sunup to sundown) at a more comfortable temperature. Since we tend to dump heat by opening the windows if overheating does occur, the hot-shot method will actually store less heat than the moderate method. Moderation works better and is more comfortable.

Figure 64 Warm surfaces radiate heat at a wavelength that is dependent upon the temperature of the radiating surface.

Selective Surfaces

There are special surfaces that can be applied to glass that enhance its ability to bring in sunlight. These commercial products are now coming on the market and may prove to have some fine uses. However, it is the more ordinary type of selective surface with which we should become more familiar.

Glass is a selective surface all by itself. Sunlight (or at least most of it,) goes right through glass. That's why we make windows out of it. Glass lets in the light, and stops the wind, and that's a good combination. Interestingly, that isn't all it will stop. It will stop some kinds of radiant energy.

The radiant heat from the sun is "hot" radiant. Its wavelength is very short, very near to that of visible light. The wavelength of the radiant heat depends upon the temperature of the surface from whence it comes. Hot sun = short wavelength.

Anything that is warm gives off warmth in the form of radiant heat. Things that are cooler than the sun, like the interior of homes and even people, give off heat which has a longer wavelength than that which comes from the sun. Glass is selective in that it will pass sunlight, but it will ABSORB and REFLECT this long wavelength light. Surprisingly, this is a very minor factor in producing the greenhouse effect, (that is, it gets hot in a greenhouse if the sun is out,) the major reason is that the glass simply keeps the wind from blowing the captured heat away. Inside the home however, the selectivity of other surfaces has a dramatic effect on the over-all operation of the home.

When a sunbeam enters through a window and lands on something, it is broken up into various parts. Some of it will be reflected, and the rest will be absorbed. Some of it which is absorbed will be conducted or convected away. That which is not taken away is either stored or re-radiated.

This sunlit surface is much cooler than the sun. Therefore it re-radiates "cool" heat; heat of a much longer wavelength than the sunlight which originally warmed the surface. This cool heat is of interest to us because we can use all sorts of selective surfaces to control where it goes, and what it does when it gets there.

Let's consider the flat black surface. Flat black has some serious draw-backs when used as it usually is, in too many solar homes. It will absorb more heat than any other color, (except some fancy commercial selective coatings). Its great absorption actually causes more problems than it cures. Mainly, because it gets hot, too hot. Walk out on black pavement with your bare feet some sunny day: it gets too hot. When used indoors it gets even hotter. It fries the green plants and is uncomfortable to be near. Also, in most of the applications I've seen, it's ugly!

What is more important, the over-all operation of a home can be greatly ENHANCED by paying closer attention to this long-wave radiant heat, and the colors it comes from.

White Works Better than Black

Commonly, solar homes are made with a large black masonry thermal mass behind a wall of glass. At first this may seem like the way to do it, in spite of the discomfort it causes. However, let me refer you to an interesting book. The Passive Solar Energy Book, by Edward Mazria pages 139-143 and 288 of the "expanded professional edition" reveal a very interesting bit of information.

Two cases are examined. While they do not have the great massiveness of the underground homes that I have discussed, nor do they take into account the whole year's accumulation of heat, they do teach us some very fine lessons.

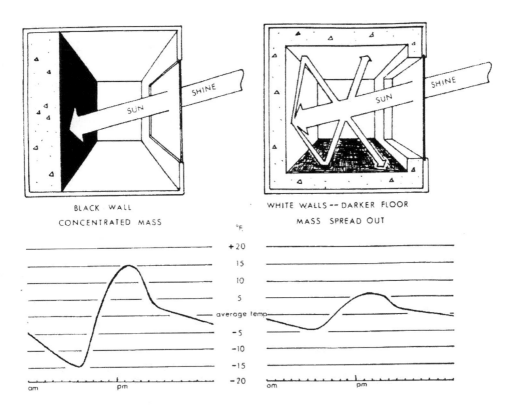

Figure 65 White works better than black as can be seen from a comparison of their temperature swings.

The first case (Figure 65) shows a home with a black masonry wall and sunshine on it in the winter. Notice that the daily temperature swing is 40°F (22.2°C). This is the usual way solar homes are, at present, being built.

The second case has the same thermal mass SPREAD OUT over the entire interior surface of the home, and all the walls and ceiling painted a LIGHT color, with a darker floor, but not black. The sun shines, not on the dark floor, but on the light walls. This simple arrangement drops the daily temperature swing to only 13°F (7.2°C)! Note though, that the author says that, if the same space were constructed with wood and sheet rock as in the usual framed manner the temperature fluctuation would be a whopping 38°F (21.1°C) instead of just 13°F (7.2°C), because these materials are light weight by comparison. So by re-arranging the materials, the temperature fluctuation in this house has gone from one which is intolerable to one which is quite comfortable!

Why? The walls are painted a light color, like good ol' contractor's off-white. Sunlight falling on it does not heat it up to an uncomfortable level as with a black wall. Most of the heat is NOT concentrated on one wall, which would also raise the temperature, but is spread out BY REFLECTION to the rest of the room. The thermal mass, which is spread around as it would be in an earth sheltered home, presents THREE TIMES as much surface area for capturing the heat than you would have by confining it to one wall. Increasing its surface also provides much greater conductive access to the heat-storing thermal mass, which allows it to do a better job of narrowing the temperature swing.

The higher temperatures do not speed things up as much as one might think because the moderation effect of the massive wall causes it to soak up its heat very slowly. A good example of this occurs when you heat up a pan of stew. If you turn on the stove to medium, and are patient, the whole pan of stew will be heated in a surprisingly short time. However, if you turn up the heat to high, the top of the stew will remain cold, while the bottom will be scorched. The first way is far better for both the thermal mass of the wall, and the thermal mass of the stew. (Of course, you could stir the stew, but it's not as easy to stir a concrete wall!)

At first one might think that there would be greater heat loss through the windows with this second method because the black wall has been removed and replaced with a white surface which COULD bounce the heat right back outside. Actually, it would have less. The angle of reflection from a white wall is not like a mirror, which would put the sunlight right back outside. Instead it spreads the heat all around to be absorbed inside the home. However, the higher temperatures produced by the black wall variety actually increases the daytime temperature differential from one side of each window to its other, which results in a greater over-all heat loss. Not to mention that it causes overheating, which would cause us to dump valuable heat.

Any surface is selective. Changing the color is one of the easiest ways to change its selective properties. Not only does a black wall absorb more sunlight than a white wall, it also radiates more of the low temperature heat. Note this though: A WHITE wall will absorb about THE SAME AMOUNT OF LOW TEMPERATURE HEAT AS A BLACK WALL. That means that once the sunlight has had its wavelength re-arranged by the surfaces it hits, that low temperature heat will be absorbed by the WHOLE HOUSE. After all, if the sunlight were not absorbed rather quickly by a white room, it would stay light inside long after the sun goes down!

The slightly darker floor will have a slightly warmer temperature. This helps balance out the rising effect of convection, and as one noted author put it, "warm feet are happy feet."* I like brown earth tones. They absorb about half as much sunlight as does flat black, they are prettier, and more comfortable. Now, I didn't say that the floor HAD TO BE brown. It is just one of many fine choices.

Did you notice what happened at the same time that we made the home work better? For one thing, it became more comfortable. More importantly, it became MORE PLEASANT to be in. Nothing will make any room feel like a cave faster, than painting the walls black! LIGHT. LIGHT. LIGHT! Lots of light. Light colored walls are more cheery.

Light colored walls and ceiling reflect more of the visible light, which makes the whole place a much nicer home. LIGHT COLORED WALLS WORK BETTER!

Why Not Carpet Anyway?!

Most authors discourage the use of carpet on the floor because it cuts down on the surface area for heat absorption and interferes with the ability of the thermal mass to do its job. I like carpet! Most people I've talked to like carpet. Isn't there a way we could be happy, and not mess up what we are trying to do thermally?

There sure is. If one designs a house that's on the verge of not working, as with the winter-oriented passive solar homes, one cannot afford the luxury of carpet from a thermal standpoint. And at the cost of carpet nowadays your pocketbook may not be able to afford it either. But, if enough features are included in the home to handle the heat flow we CAN keep our carpet. After all, should a home's performance be measured only in BTU's? Shouldn't it rather be measured in usefulness and comfort? What happens to the radiant heat that is not absorbed by the carpet when the sun shines on it? It's reflected. Is it wasted? No, it's just absorbed somewhere else in the home. That which is absorbed is either re-radiated to be absorbed by the white walls, or is conducted away by the floor underneath. (Not much is stored in the carpet.) The R-value of carpet is only about 1 or 2 (0.08 or 1 metric R) for the whole thickness, so not very much insulation is really being added, if you consider the entire interior surface of the home. What insulation value there is, is usually shorted out by conduction through masonry walls and concrete floor anyway. In the Geodome the temperature under the carpeted floor is the same as it is behind the masonry walls.

Any time part of the conductive surface inside the home is insulated with anything, the ability of the earth around the home to receive and return the heat is impaired. An actual carpeted masonry surface (including concrete) will absorb only 44% of the heat that a bare concrete floor will. The efficiency will be reduced to about 25% for those few places where the sun shines on the floor. Adding carpet is therefore, a compromise in the thermal operation of the home. This is a compromise for comfort that can be satisfactorily made up by providing plenty of other conductive surfaces for the heat to use.

I also hate concrete floors, they make my feet hurt. A well designed convective-heat-flow system will also allow for heat storage under a wooden floor without having to use a hard surface. It will also work without the loss in efficiency because of the carpet; convection can simply carry the heat around the floor. Then any surface you like, carpet or not, will work just fine. Also, the carpet on plastic, on dry earth, suggested in the interesting book: $50 and Up Underground House Book should provide a reasonably good over-all thermal connection.

So, design a good home and enjoy your carpet.

Mean Radiant Temperature

While you are standing on your carpet in the middle of your home radiating heat, the home is radiating heat back. You can actually feel it, but you are used to it and may not notice what is happening. The temperature of the walls and the air temperature may not be the same, but there is a variety of combinations that will still feel comfortable.

The average wall temperature at which this heat is radiated is called the mean radiant temperature. If the walls are cold, the air must be much warmer so that one will feel comfortable. If the walls, and thus the mean radiant temperature, are WARM, the air should be much cooler for us to be comfortable. The earth sheltered home tends to have both the air and the walls at about the same temperature. The temperature at which most people are comfortable with, wall and air, are the same, is 68°F (20°C). People are individuals though, so the exact temperature that you prefer will probably differ some.

Most of the literature I've seen on the subject discusses the situation where the walls are cold. Most homes in the north, where people are at all concerned about mean radiant temperature, have cold walls. Usually the warm wall situation does not arise. However, the Geodome has warm walls. Under certain conditions you can actually feel the radiant heat from the ceiling on the backs of your hands. Turn them over and you feel it on your palms. The sensation is very slight, but detectable.

I felt that the Geodome was more comfortable at 66°F (19°C). "Nitpicking" one might say but interesting nevertheless. As more homes are build using Passive Annual Heat Storage we should learn much more about the effects of mean radiant temperature, and how it changes the actual temperature where we will be most comfortable. However, the individual feelings of each person may play a more important role in determining how each home should work than any generalized statement about what the mean radiant temperature should be.

Happily, the actual operational temperature of a Passive Annual Heat Storage home is adjustable so you may set it where you like it, mean radiant temperature and all.

Notes:

Chapter 9 – Adjusting the Earth's Constant Temperature

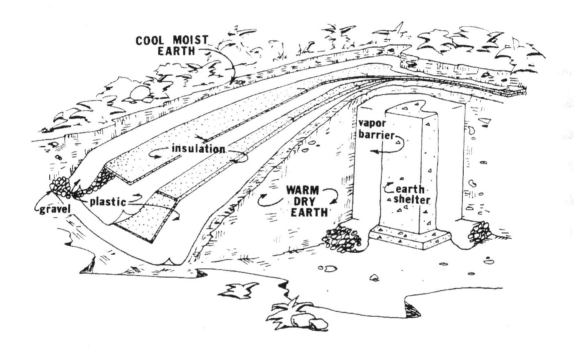

The Geodome

The Geodome (the working example of Chapter 1) is a fine stepping-stone between the conventional earth shelter and a full Passive Annual Heat Storage home. It is the earliest and longest operating example of long-term heat storage. There are several major points that we may learn from the way it works.

1. Temperature changes occur very slowly.
2. The existence of the solar-heated earth-sheltered home in the earth environment will raise the deep-earth temperature.
3. The home will "float" at a higher temperature than the indigenous deep-earth temperature.

4. The deep-earth constant temperature can be modified to a depth of at least 12 feet (3.7 meters) by adjusting the indoor average annual air temperature.

5. The surrounding earth may be heated sufficiently so that heat will re-enter the home whenever the indoor temperature attempts to fall.

6. That insulation does not have to encase the entire thermal mass to be used for warm heat storage.

7. The earth environment will remain dry under the insulation/watershed umbrella.

8. The water control measures in sensitive areas are important.

Hind-sight is always 20/20. So there are some important things that we may learn from the way it does NOT work. While it has been operating sufficiently to test the theory, a modern Passive Annual Heat Storage home would have some distinctly different features.

The Geodome's average annual air temperature is about 68°F (20°C), which means that it will drop down to the mid or even low 60's (high teens Celsius) in the winter. If this is considered unacceptably low for the home owner, then the only method available for raising that temperature is to turn on the back up heat. This is exactly what occurred during the second winter of operation. While the energy use was small, just about the same amount as was used by the electric hot water heater, it still had to be paid for.

Properly, the Passive Annual Heat Storage home should be made so that more sunshine would enter the home during the warmer times of the year. Very little can be done in this case; the windows are too small. The windows don't spread the heat out properly over the day-long collecting time, and most importantly, the major shading devices are solidly fixed in place; they are not adjustable.

Underground there are also several improvements to be made. The insulation/watershed umbrella extends out only 10 feet (3 meters) beyond the footing, and is not properly tapered, as discussed in Chapter 4. Therefore the outdoor temperatures still have too great a role in determining what the underground temperature will be. No doubt, the round shape of the building which allows more dirt on the roof, and the two story height, which puts the entire home deeper into the earth, has helped greatly in making it work as well as it has.

Structurally separate, but attached to the Geodome, is a two story Quonset-hut-shaped section of the home which has two extra bedrooms, a bath, garage, and spa room. It has two sliding glass doors, and a 16-foot (4.9-meter) garage door, which present a very great heat loss because they face northwest. Along the south side of this extra section, the umbrella has been inadvertently chopped back to within about four feet of the building. The main dome is generally blocked off from these other rooms, so that there isn't a proper free flow of air and heat from the main house. All of these things together have caused the expected larger temperature fluctuations, in these other rooms, sometimes reaching even into the low 60's (high teens Celsius).

While a modern Passive Annual Heat Storage home would be built somewhat differently, the Geodome is important from a testing standpoint because:

1. It shows the importance of keeping the umbrella and the Isolation Zone sufficiently large.

2. It demonstrates how all parts of the home should function together as a unified heat-control system.

3. It allows us the opportunity to learn more than if it all worked perfectly. It tells us where we can skimp, and where we cannot.

4. It shows how important it is that a Passive Annual Heat Storage home should be ADJUSTABLE.

The Geodome is another "giant" whose shoulders we can now climb upon, so we can peer even further into the principles of Passive Annual Heat Storage.

Slowly – Very Slowly

Adjusting the deep-earth constant temperature takes a lot of time. It takes three years to fully climatize the soil around the home. Yet, after the first nice warm summer the home should be quite close to its final floating temperature, and reasonably comfortable, although some auxiliary heat may be needed that first winter. The completed home can be heated during this interim by a stove, wood or otherwise, just as quickly as any other home of its size. It will not lose heat very rapidly since it is inherently very energy efficient. Heat that goes into the earth is not lost, but stored. The earth will soak up the heat, but very slowly. Hence, any changes we hope to make will also occur VERY SLOWLY.

Bringing a large body of earth up to temperature still takes a very large amount of heat. Since no one wants to pay for all that heat, the home is solar heated. It is this free solar heat, taken in over a very long time, which is used to raise the temperature of all that earth.

If, at the time of construction, the earth is at its warmest anyway, (the first part of September,) or if you have a whole summer ahead of you before the next winter, then there is plenty of both time and heat for that first winter's needs. However, if you have the earth open to the cold winter air during construction, it will cool off. The result is that it not only takes more heat, and thus more time to climatize your new home, but you have a long wait before that free heat will again be available. All that earth can store "cold" just as well as its stores heat.

The Institute of the Rockies

In the late fall of 1981 the Geodome was proving itself very effective and it was becoming increasingly evident that we had accomplished a breakthrough.

John Badgley of the Institute of the Rockies, (no relation to the Rocky Mountain Research Center but very helpful to us nevertheless,) approached me to re-design the insulation for their underground conference center. This interesting building was under construction and half way buried already; a nasty time to be making changes.

Its conventional earth-shelter design clearly indicated that the building would be over-heated all summer and under-heated all winter. Even with the first floor subterranean walls already insulated and backfilled, the decision was made to make some changes anyway in the hopes of up-grading its operation.

A small wing type umbrella (similar to the one described in Chapter 4) was added, while the 2nd floor, rear walls were left uninsulated. The roof system was not designed to hold the weight of any added Storage Zone so the one and a half feet (46 centimeters) of Moderation Zone from the original design was retained. 8-foot (2.4-meter) wings were added on the sides and rear of the building. This is smaller than desirable, but the two story depth gives quite a bit more isolation than a single story would have, and the trees behind the building seemed to be worth saving. (An umbrella around a tree will cause it to die of thirst.)

Unfortunately, the building wasn't completed that winter, having NO insulation on the large exposed face. However, the earth kept things from freezing up. In fact, it maintained a temperature of about 50°F (10°C).

All that next summer it cooled itself, putting away lots of heat for the following winter. In spite of the fact that the insulation had yet to be installed, the temperature was staying in the mid 60's (high teens C). by the middle of September, even after a few freezing nights. Four feet (1.2 meters) behind the north wall, the Storage Zone was 71°F (22°C).

However, the exposed face must be properly insulated, or else all it has saved will continue to blow away in the winter wind.

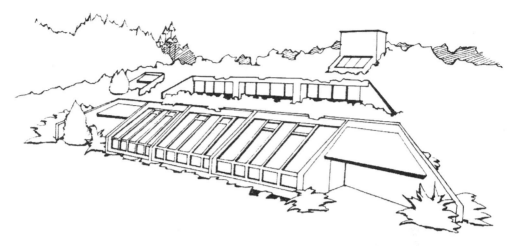

Figure 66 The Institute of the Rockies underground conference center.

The fact that the temperature 4 feet behind the wall was 71°F (22°C) is significant because it proves, as did the Geodome, that the earth around an underground building can actually be heated up as I have described. Even this uncompleted building, which throws away its heat in the winter, provides such proof. The earth around a conventional earth shelter does not get warm enough, deep enough, so that the stored heat can return over a long enough period of time, because the heat-storing earth is insulated from the heat-collecting house, and because the usual underground home is shaded from the required summer sun.

Happily, the over-heating threat (and it was a big one,) has been completely cured. It was comfortable all summer and at no time was it necessary to vent any heat.

So remember, it takes a heap o' heat to change the earth's constant temperature, and a long time to gather it.

The Annual Balance of Heat Flow

Out in an open field the total amount of heat going into the earth all summer is perfectly balanced with the amount of heat coming out all winter. Thus the deep-earth constant temperature is the same as the average annual air temperature. This is the ANNUAL BALANCE OF HEAT FLOW. If that balance is altered, the deep-earth temperature will gradually change.

The earth sheltered home itself will be used to accomplish the necessary alteration of the annual balance of heat flow. Our home will then be immersed snugly into the newly climatized earth.

We would like to raise the deep-earth temperature by about 25°F (14°C) or so here in Montana, that's from 45°F to about 70°F (7°C to about 21°C). Modifying the annual balance of heat flow will change the average annual air temperature inside the earth sheltered home, and will therefore change the deep-earth temperature.

Here are the basic adjustment principles we can use:

1. The home will be a thermal one-way door. Over the WHOLE YEAR, it must let IN more heat than it lets OUT.
2. The layout of windows and other types of solar collectors should provide a fairly constant heat supply throughout the DAY, so the home may soak up the heat slowly without over-heating.
3. Provide earth tubes for heat storage and removal as well as for fresh air.
4. Conduction through ALL underground surfaces is essential, so do not cover over major portions of the interior surfaces with insulation (note the exception of carpet discussed in Chapter 8).
5. Make sure you have a well-designed convective connection between the radiant heat coming in and the conductive surfaces which will take it into and out of storage.
6. Implement all the principles on heat flow and control described throughout this book.
7. Then MAKE IT ADJUSTABLE.

Adjustment Through the Basic Layout

By putting windows on more than just the south side, including some east and/or west windows too, you'll spread the daily sunlight over a longer time than with the "hot shot" all south method. Don't worry if you can't put them on all three sides. After-all, the Geodome has only its south and northwest sides open. Just do what you can.

Except in Australia, (south of the equator,) the north side seems to be the likely place for earthen heat storage. The rest of the basic layout is up to you if you keep in mind the internal heat flow requirements.

The existence of this specially designed house in the earth environment will naturally raise the constant temperature of its surrounding earth, and is the biggest of all the "adjustments." All else is just fine tuning.

Fine Tuning: Making the Year-Round Constant Temperature Adjustable

To fine tune the home's final floating temperature, we need to be able to ADJUST the ANNUAL BALANCE OF HEAT FLOW so that we can either raise or lower the "constant" temperature. We have, therefore, two ways of accomplishing this. ONE, by letting more heat in, and TWO, by letting more heat out.

Whatever adjustments you make, do it so as to make yourself MORE COMFORTABLE. Electronic thermostats and mechanical controls or the like, are usually completely superfluous because the changes occurs so very slowly. YOU are the thermostat, and you have plenty of time to make any needed adjustments.

For the more exacting person, a few key places should be monitored—like inside the home, outside the home, the Storage Zone next to the wall, and half way out under the umbrella, maybe even the Moderation Zone, Isolation Zone, and a little ways into the end of each earth tube if you can. Keep track of exactly where the temperature sensors are located and what their temperatures are.

If it seems to be too hot 10 feet into the Storage Zone, it must have been too hot inside the house THREE MONTHS AGO; too late for an adjustment now. Since the temperatures which occur inside affect the soil, and take a long time to soak in, the temperatures at various depths are thermal history written into the earth. So, don't panic if its 70°F degrees (21°C), ten feet behind the wall, on the first of September when the hottest it's been in the house all summer is only 74°F (23°C). It will not get up to 115°F (46°C) back there - it can only reach 74°F (23°C). Be patient.

Whatever you wish the AVERAGE ANNUAL INDOOR TEMPERATURE to be, adjust the inside temperature to be about 3°F or 4°F (1.5°C or 2°C) higher in the summertime. The whole structure should swing only about 6°F to 8°F (3.3°C to 4.4°C) all year. The better your design turns out, the narrower the temperature deviation. Therefore, it you wish it to remain about 68°F (20°C) in the wintertime, adjust the summertime temperature to about 74°F (23°C).

Controlling the Heat Input

How do you adjust it? FIRST: by controlling the heat input. This is simply accomplished by shading the windows more to turn the temperature down and by letting in more sunlight if it needs to warm up. SECONDLY: by adjusting the heat output. If your design has a terrible (and it would have to be really terrible) over heating problem, only then would you want to vent it.

To let in more heat we need bigger windows. If your windows are too small, you'll have to bust a hole in the wall to make them bigger. If they are slightly oversized you can provide outside shades of various kinds and cut the solar input down. (If you're clever, put the adjustment handle inside, and the shade outside.) But how big should the windows be?

Here in Montana "winter oriented" passive homes are said to require the same amount of window area as 50% of their floor space. That is, a 1,000 square foot home should have about 500 square feet of glass. The Geodome has only 6.6% of its 3,380 square feet in actual glass, yet it performed superbly under the circumstances. It just happened to hit it at about the lower limit, but it is not adjustable. 15% to 25% would be better.

The exact size the windows should be is another of those things that the pioneering work in Passive Annual Heat Storage has yet to establish. The large expanse of glass customary with winter-oriented solar homes would clearly be un-needed when the heat is collected over the entire year. Such over-sized windows would also present an unacceptably high winter's heat loss, and would thus require large expensive thermal shutters or some other way of keeping the heat in during the winter. The earth though, is forgiving and therefore, we do not have to be too precise. The windows should be big enough so we can shade, and adjust the sunlight coming in, but smaller than required in your area for the now antiquated winter-oriented passive solar home. But DON'T NAIL ON an overhang as is done in winter-oriented passive solar because things which are nailed-on are NOT ADJUSTABLE. Besides, you will want MORE heat in the spring and LESS in the fall even though the sun is at the SAME angle.

If overheating does occur, turn down the sun first, before you vent any of those precious BTUs. There are a number of fine shading methods including: shutters, louvers, and awnings. They have only two thermal requirements. They should be ADJUSTABLE, and they should make shade! So, if it gets too hot, make more shade. If it gets too cold, let in more light.

Ordinarily the shading device would be added to the outside of the windows because inside shades do not work as well. Once inside, the heat must then be moved back outside, and even with reflective shades a substantial portion of it will already be captured by convection and trapped inside. However, a well-designed home will be able to store a very substantial amount of heat, much more than would probably be left over after interior blinds are shut. This would indicate that indoor blinds would work fine, although it may become too dark inside or one may not recognize that overheating is about to occur until it's too hot for comfort. Try it! A home that is good at storing excess heat will cool down to a comfortable level very quickly when you close the shades, or will simply not get hot enough to be uncomfortable. So, don't toss the idea. It may work well for you.

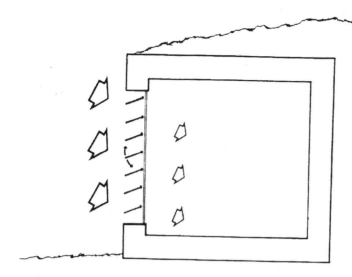

**Figure 67
Controlling the heat
input** by using
adjustable shading
devices.

Controlling the Heat Output

The exposed portion of the home is where the major heat output will occur. Naturally, this exposed face should be well insulated, have good thermal breaks and use dual pane windows. (Avoid high-e glass, it works backwards for this use.) Most climates, except maybe in the Yukon, do not need triple-pane.

Removable insulation for the windows is a good way to control the night time heat loss, although it will probably only be needed in the extreme weather. (They never got around to making the ones for the Geodome—it went the whole year without any!) In designs with extensive convection ducts, envelopes and the like, a means of preventing reverse air flow is good. The basic goal is to prevent heat loss unless it is intentional.

If overheating occurs and you must dump heat, two openings are required. Two windows at the same level for cross ventilation, if the wind is blowing. Or a low vented window, and a skylight for convective removal. Also, some people like to leave a bedroom window open at night. All of these methods should work well.

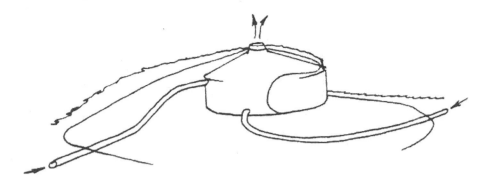

Figure 68 Using both earth tubes to raise the earth temperature with the warm outside air, while allowing excess internal heat to power the convective flow.

Adjusting with Earth Tubes

Earth tubes provide us with an opportunity to either lower or raise the deep-earth temperature. Warm summer air is an excellent source of heat. Nearly everywhere there is at least a little. Since we generally wish to cool that air anyway before it enters the home, it only seems logical that its heat should be put away for later use.

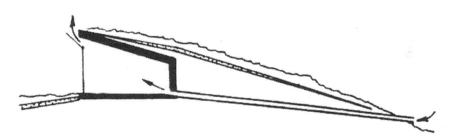

Figure 69 Dumping heat to remove excess heat can lower the indoor temperature, and if it's warm outside, raise the temperature of the earth around the tubes.

Convectively powered earth tubes eliminate many of the problems that occur with the other earth tube arrangements because they are self-adjusting. The more ventilation is needed the harder they work, even if the temperature is dropping rather than rising.

Most installations will use passive solar as the primary heat source. In this case the tubes will automatically store the excess heat as it enters the through the windows. This storage occurs around the upper earth tube. Naturally, warm summer outdoor air will have its heat stored around the lower earth tube as it enters.

Interestingly, the cool morning air will NOT be cooled further, as it would in a mechanical air conditioning unit. Why? Much of the night, heat is being taken out of storage rather than being put in, which means that the air is being warmed as it goes the other way. This keeps the earth on the inside end of the lower tube at room temperature, while keeping the cold wave-front away from the home so the air entering will always be comfortable. To put it simply, the air which enters the tubes has its temperature MODERATED. When the air is warm it is automatically cooled, then it is cool it is automatically warmed. So, even in the morning when the sun is out but the air is cool, the incoming fresh air will be comfortable.

This general earth tube arrangement (Figure 46) is made to keep the inside within a narrow temperature range. We can, however, raise the midpoint of that range over a very long period of time. This can be accomplished by forcing air through the tubes when it's hot outside. Likewise, the mid-point temperature may be lowered when it's cool outside.

If a skylight, clearstory, or other high window were to be opened, AND if the sun is shining into the home, convection powered by the sunlight coming in the windows, would draw air through BOTH earth tubes. The air would enter at room temperature, which would seem cool and comfortable on a hot summer's day, but its heat would be deposited in the earth around BOTH earth tubes. This heat input would have the effect of gradually increasing the temperature in the Storage Zone without running that heat through the house. But heat would be stored just as it is when the sun shines in, except that it takes that heat from the air.

Any one of a number of solar chimney designs could be constructed to accomplish essentially the same thing for those cases where direct sunlight is limited, but would be available to the solar chimney.

However, an open skylight will not draw air through the earth tubes if a door or window is open in the house, this works only because the house is tight.

If the skylight were opened at night, whether winter, summer or any time the outdoor air is cool, heat will be continually dumped out of the house, the Storage Zone, and the counterflow heat exchange sections of earth around the earth tubes. Therefore, if you wish to cool the entire system, dump heat at night.

The balance of heat flow can also be altered by using electric fans. Fans have the advantage of being available as an option when a less than optimum design is used, especially when retrofitting an older building (see Chapter 10). An exhaust fan on the ceiling will blow hot air outside, pulling air through the earth tubes as it would when using convection. But if the air inside is not uncomfortable, then the exhaust fan should NOT be located ON THE CEILING, but AT OR BELOW FLOOR LEVEL. This way heat will be added to the earthen heat Storage Zone on the outer end of the earth tube without taking it away from the inside. Basically, we must blow the warm summer air through the tubes without making it uncomfortable inside.

At night too, fans can be used to blow cool air through the tubes to cool off the earthen heat Storage Zone if we wish.

Also, the tubes can be fitted with one-way plastic flapper doors. This would cause a deliberate imbalance to occur, over a long period of time, having the effect of heating up or cooling off the earth depending on which way that "one way" was. If it only allows air to go into the top tube from the inside, then the Storage Zone will gradually heat up from the heat which collects in the house. If it allows air to escape from the top tube (as viewed from the inside) then it will gradually cool the Storage Zone.

Reversible fans could have a similar effect, especially if your arrangement doesn't lend itself very well to convective flow, such as with retro-fitted above-ground homes.

Remember though, we are just fine tuning it. In most climates the basic Passive Annual Heat Storage arrangement should already operate at or near 70°F (21° C), which means that MOST homes will need little or no adjustment. So don't go overboard on adjusting. But if you use the principles that provide this ability, you will be better equipped to handle a greater variety of home designs, and will be able to make Passive Annual Heat Storage work much better for you.

Under Heating?

The principles described here will enhance just about any design even if your conditions are extreme, or design limitations severe. But, what if your design under heats? Re-read this book or use back-up heat! Certainly, you shouldn't need very much!

Chapter 10 – The Earth Shelter Pioneer

Kindling Imagination's Spark

Innovation is procreative. Conception occurs with the spark of a new idea in the imagination of the fireside pioneer and one idea begets another. The matchmaker collects innovation from all over into a treasure chest of parent ideas. Collectively, the new and the old give birth to a fresh outlook, which in turn can become father to even better methods in the future. Hopefully this publication will prove to be a matchmaker, for there is much still ahead of us.

Before you begin learning by busting your knuckles, and we all must learn some things that way, take all of your ideas and put them into one design. But don't build that one. Nail it up on the wall where you can see it, and begin designing your second one, your third and your fourth.

The experience gained on each is very valuable, and besides, paper is much cheaper than building first and then remodeling.

It was once said that "experience is the best teacher, but sometimes you learn things you didn't want to know!" We can all learn from our successes, but we have much to learn from our mistakes too. Study all you can of the progress and the miscalculations through which others have forged their way. For, like Sir Isaac, we too are "standing on the shoulders of giants."

Keeping a Journal

For most people, just remembering what has happened and why, is an impossible task. Therefore, I'd recommend keeping a journal from day one. Keep a record of the reasons for the design decisions that you have made. Then, as you make others, you'll be able to review the reasons that got you where you are. For soon you will discover when you tug on the tail of your homemade animal, the head will waggle. So many things become interdependent that you'll want to go back and review the reasons that brought you where you are. Then you may revise those reasons if you are not satisfied with where you wound up.

Next, keep track of the construction progress and match it to your prearranged sequence of events. Building a house is like solving a Rubik's Cube. You must accomplish each step in its proper order or the whole thing gets messed up.

Your journal will become especially useful as you monitor the operation of your new abode. Remember now, it responds VERY SLOWLY. Writing down your observations, both good and bad, will allow you to see if what you suspect may be happening is really underway or not. For example, say one of your windows leaks. Trace back the water-flow to see where it came from in the first place. Try to find out, not just how it happened, but why it happened. Then jot down these reasons so that things may be designed a little better next time. We want our views to be continually corrected like a sailing ship which must tack back and forth in order to make any progress into the wind. If we do not actually correct our understanding the design improvement process jumps all over like a tin can when you kick it down the street!

The design decisions you make, even the details, will determine the total result. The sum of its parts may produce the most advanced home ever, or you may have other priorities with other results. You may not, for example, achieve full annual heat storage in your first design. You may not wish to. You may have wished to, but other things got in the way. That is the life of a designer. But using these new tools can certainly extend the time your home can go without heat, make it more comfortable, enjoyable, and efficient, and improve whatever you are planning to make.

The experience of others who have written books is that they soon become snowed with a deluge of questions. So please go over this entire book first. Your question may have already been answered. If you do write, we would certainly appreciate a stamped self-addressed envelope, and a tax deductible contribution to cover our time. For the more serious, we can offer certain design and design assistance services as time and circumstances permit.

However things turn out, we would like to hear from you. The greater the amount of info that you are willing to share with us, the more we can all learn together, which in turn may lead to future publications. For every writer with an experience or a question there are probably a thousand with the same question who didn't write.

Please visit us online at www.EarthShelters.com

Any new idea provides lots of room for innovation, and now this book has laid out the principles to put you on the road to further invention. What may be on that road? Here are some things that are on the horizon.

Fire Control

Many earth shelters have been built because they tend to be safer from natural disasters, among them, fire. Earth doesn't burn! In fact, even a thin layer of dirt will offer protection from fast moving forest and brush fires.

How tragic it was to see the many homes in California that have been lost because of flammable roofs and gale driven brush fires. Just an inch (2.5 centimeters) of moist dirt on their roofs could have saved many of them. But don't put on more than an inch (2.5 centimeters) or so because you'll cave in the roof. Just hosing down the roof doesn't work because it all evaporates in the intense heat. But moist earth will stay intact in most winds, while dry earth may be blown away.

However, this all takes time! If you've waited too long and the fire is close by, time HAS run out: SCRAM! You can always build a subterranean home with the insurance money.

Hot Water Warm Up

If you pipe in your cold water through 20 feet (6 meters) of 70°F (21°C) earth, how much cold water will you drink? So, strange as it may seem, insulate your COLD water pipe all the way into the house and keep it cold.

BTU's used to heat domestic hot water are measured in DOLLARS. So the more heat dollars you can get for free the better. Now, it takes the same amount of heat to raise a cup of water from 45°F to 70°F (7°C to 21°C) as it does from 70°F to 95°F (21°C to 35°C). And again that amount up to 120°F (49°C). Therefore, if you can raise it the first third for free, you should save about a third on your water heating bill. (Even conventional underground homes use more power to heat the water than they do to heat the house.)

How can you clip off a third of your (now) biggest bill? By plumbing a loop of pipe back into the warm storage earth to pre-heat your water to 70°F (21°C) before it enters the hot water tank, solar heater or whatever. Depending on circumstances, it should go for quite a ways, maybe 20 or 30 feet (6 or 9 meters), right next to the house in the warmest part of the earth. The pipe should also be located at least 20 feet (6 meters) of conductive path away from the exposed surface and as close as possible to places where a goodly amount of heat is being put into storage. Where the sun shines on a near-by wall or has a direct convection connection to the solar input would be excellent choices. At first, you will probably want to operate for a length of time without it, and then for a while with it to see what effect it may have.

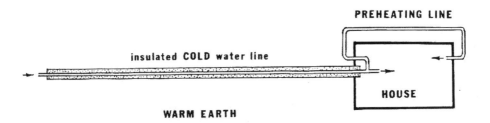

PREHEATING LINE

insulated COLD water line

HOUSE

WARM EARTH

Figure 70 Preheating domestic hot water with free stored heat.

You may wish to include a by-pass to cut it out in the event that you're taking out more heat than you would like which would make the wall cold. However, you should not use a direct by-pass valve. The valve itself will short out your heating loop. It would be better to use a pair of shut off valves, and a short removable piece of pipe with union type connections. That way, when the loop is in use, there will be no backward heat flow. (Figure 70)

Remember, insulate the COLD pipe NOT THE HOT ONE.

Yukon to the Amazon

The basic Passive Annual Heat Storage principles are applicable to buildings in almost any climate. The primary requisite is a summer/winter temperature difference and enough sunlight in the WARM season to allow collection of sufficient heat. Those few places that haven't any appreciable temperature changes (like tropical islands) are the most difficult, but are nevertheless challenging candidates for heat or cold storage.

How about the far, far north? (Or south for that matter?) Do they not receive many more hours of sunshine in the summer? Yes, it's much colder in the winter, but it is the summertime that provides the heat.

In such arctic climates, the insulation umbrella may have to be increased in both thickness and earth coverage area, and the minimum Isolation Zone increased. But, there is certainly no reason to expect the above outlined principles of physics to suddenly become invalid just because the temperatures are extreme and spread apart in time. Design freedom may be somewhat limited. Window insulation, extra thick thermal breaks, and the like will probably be required, along with paying close attention to all thermal details. Certainly, if anywhere, cold climates should be a natural for Passive Annual Heat Storage. Montana isn't exactly the banana belt of the world, ya know!

Permafrost may be the biggest problem. Some locations in the tundra will not allow for the melting of the permafrost. It turns into a sea of mud! The soil must be solid (when warm) and able to support the weight of the home after the permafrost melts, because it will melt.

Lowering the Constant Temperature

What if your average annual air temperature is higher than 70°F (21°C)? You can still use the Passive Annual Heat Storage principles to produce a constant climate environment with a LOWER temperature. To accomplish this, instead of heating it up all summer with solar energy, you must DUMP HEAT whenever it is cool outside. The earth tubes provide the greatest opportunity for providing a cool environment.

Upside-Down Earth Tubes

What would happen if the two earth tubes were put in so that they would go UP HILL OUT OF THE HOUSE, rather than downhill as shown? Instead of a heat trap you have a COLD TRAP. All winter long, heat would be dumped outside, continually cooling off the earth. If this is your goal, you would NOT want solar gain through the windows, but would shade them and/or face them to the north.

The actual operational temperature would be somewhere between the average annual air temperature and the coldest temperature of the winter. How cold depends on your design and the available conditions. However, in fairly warm climates it should be adjustable to a comfortable level. But what if such an arrangement is used in COLD climates?

In the old days, ice was cut from rivers and lakes, and stored all summer with just a foot of sawdust for insulation. Consequently, it should be possible to produce a PERMANENT COLD STORAGE facility, passively. Simply do not allow any heat to enter, run cold winter air through the upside-down earth tubes when it is available, and provide the interior with an average annual air temperature as low as you would like it. If your winters are not cold enough, then this arrangement will still provide a much cooler place to start with, and can save you "tons" on mechanical cooling costs.

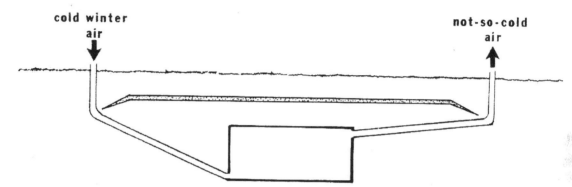

Figure 71 Upside-down earth tubes will produce a permanent cold storage when used in a climate with cold winters.

Above-Ground Retrofit

Yes, it is possible to retrofit existing homes to provide annual heat storage, or at least long-term heat storage to reduce your fuel bills. It is not easy, but it is possible. Almost EVERY HOME SITS ON THE GROUND. Every home that does sit on the ground, and is not using it for heat storage, is throwing away one of its greatest assets.

Retrofitting does not mean dumping dirt all over your home! The principles presented in this book can be used to upgrade homes, but one should first of all review some preliminary steps.

1. Review all the requirements for Passive Annual Heat Storage.
2. Determine how they may or may not be used in your case.
3. Count the cost; see if retrofitting is worth it. Doing it right in the first place is far better than trying to make a bad design work better.
4. Remember that YOU ARE THE PIONEER, and things may not turn out as well as you would like, but if you are diligent, you'll come up with a good design.

Now that you are mentally prepared, here are the physical requirements.

Retrofitting Requirements

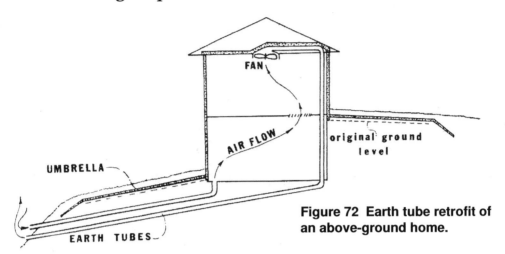

Figure 72 Earth tube retrofit of an above-ground home.

1. SUPER-INSULATE FIRST. Basement walls and masonry homes should be super-insulated on the outside. Without super-insulation and minimal infiltration, you will probably NOT achieve full annual heat storage. (Remember, I said it wouldn't be easy.)
2. Design a solar collection system to move the summer's heat into the Storage Zone. Here are some suggestions:
    a. Direct Radiation. Make the sun shine in the basement.
    b. Earth tubes made to cool the summer's hot air. Cooling the air saves the heat. Earth tubes hold the key to inexpensive retrofitting of above-ground buildings. True, it would be harder to get convection powered air through them, but clever application of heat flow principles should overcome these problems, or just use fans.
    c. Convection-connection. A well designed convection loop could connect the home to the earth storage using a very deep, insulated "cold sump."
    d. All of the above!
3. Put an umbrella ALL THE WAY AROUND the home just as if it were an earth shelter with a large exposed face. It may prove

easier to put an extra couple of feet of dirt would be the most difficult problem to overcome, as improper water control would cause rotting. You could berm further up the wall, but the earth would probably have to be made self-supporting, since regular walls won't stand the strain. Remember that the earth berm is, thermally, a part of the home. So, don't just let the wind blow between your house and some retaining wall next to it. If you have a masonry home, check with an engineer before you attempt to use it to hold back very much of an earth berm. You may also want to save the sod by rolling it up, and then putting your nice green lawn back on when the berm is in place.

4. Provide all of the water control methods of Chapter 4.

5. The home MUST have a good thermal connection between itself and the earthen Storage Zone, or else it cannot store and retrieve heat properly.

BASEMENTS are already "earth sheltered," and could provide a good thermal connection to the earth. However, you'll have to blow the heat from the top of the house down into the basement if you cannot get it down there by natural means. All the heat storage in the world will not warm up a cold basement. You must PUT heat into it. Not paid-for heat; free summer heat.

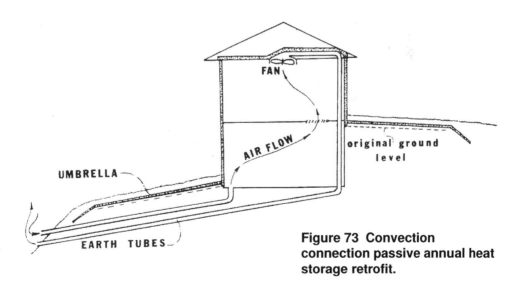

Figure 73 Convection connection passive annual heat storage retrofit.

Attics are great summertime solar collectors. I've never seen one that wasn't unbearably hot all summer. If it wasn't for those vents they put in them, some would even catch fire. Now, if you were to blow that heat into the basement... But remember to provide an automatic means for dumping that heat if your fans quit. Also, review the similar heat flow problems that have crept up in envelope homes (Chapter 6) and make your building changes sensibly.

You cannot send and receive heat from the ground if there is insulation all over the walls, inside or out. Yes, the home would have to be super-insulated, and the umbrella added around the whole building. However, you may be able to add such components one at a time, until it works as you want it to. Don't allow that 8-inch (20-centimeter) section of basement wall between the siding and the ground to remain uninsulated, bare to the air. It is that small section which has the greatest heat loss in most basements. It must be insulated down to the umbrella, but uninsulated below it.

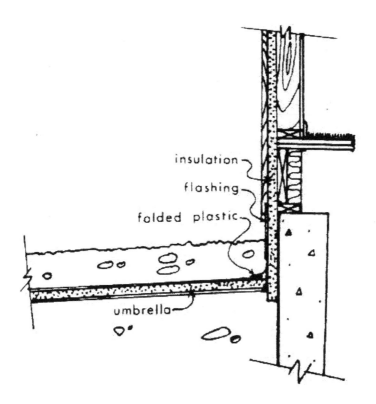

insulation

flashing

folded plastic

umbrella

Figure 74 The insulation must be continuous from the super-insulated walls all the way down to the end of the umbrella.

Green plants usually require more light than heat, so large shaded windows with winter-time/night-time insulation could produce a year-round constant climate, a 12 MONTH GROWING SEASON, in your Passive Annual Greenhouse.

The openness of a large greenhouse should allow for a good radiation and convection connection to the conductive walls. Painting everything white will allow the plants more light in the visible range, while absorbing the heat into the earth. However, the ability to store that heat would probably mean that the shading would be somewhat less since the inside temperature would not rise as quickly, if at all. But shading devices should be more adjustable than the whitewash usually used on greenhouses.

Bigger earth tubes, maybe with exhaust fans, could be installed. Both tubes could be used to exhaust the heat in the summer while allowing fresh air in the windows. Of course, your location will have quite an effect on just how and at what temperatures this would be done. Basically, a greenhouse operates at a slightly lower temperature than a house, and it has considerably more glass, with the correspondingly large winter and night time heat losses. Otherwise they function the same way.

People tend to be less concerned about the thermal design of greenhouses than regular homes, but with such a lofty goal as year-round growing, one must pay attention to every detail.

Imagine: growing oranges and pineapples in Saskatchewan.

Constant Energy Supply for Whatever

What's your pleasure?
- Low temperature or high temperature?
- Cold storage – 0°F (-18°C)
- Refrigerator – 45°F (7°C)
- Green plant comfort – 60°F (16°C)
- People comfort – 70°F (21°C)
- Hot tubs and swimming pools – 107°F (42°C)
- Domestic hot water – 120°F (49°C)
- Composting and methane generation – 125°F (52°C)
- Steam electric production – 250°F (121°C)

Yes, you can choose your temperature. Just remember that you must provide proper separation, isolation and insulation between the different temperature zones.

Do you have a periodic source of heat or cold, and you wish to use it later? Solar energy is like that, lots all summer, with the need all winter. Without annual heat storage all solar heated systems suffer from that same handicap. But need they?

Does all this seem too far out? Remember Ben Franklin's kite? What was the result?

Yes, the field of solar energy is a pan of hot buttered popcorn. You never know what may pop out next!

Passive Annual Heat Storage
takes solar energy out of the dark ages!

Appendix A

Design Guidelines for the PAHS Pioneer

These guidelines are meant to provide an overall outline and are not absolute, They should give the pioneer in passive annual heat storage a general "place to begin," in an infant science.

The Insulation/Watershed Umbrella

1. Extend umbrella out and around the entire home and above also, if the home is fully earth sheltered.
2. Extend out 20 feet (6 meters) where ever possible.
3. Taper insulation from 4 inches (10 centimeters) down to one (the first inch is the most important)
4. Insulate the backs of retaining walls and other items that will be backfilled before the main umbrella goes into place.
5. Plastic: .006 inch (.15 mm), largest sheets practical.
   a. 3 layers minimum
   b. Separate layers with soft insulation or dirt that will drain well.
   c. Provide adequate drainage out the end of the umbrella.
   d. DO NOT stretch, but allow for settling with folds and slipping over-laps.
   e. Lay like shingles.
   f. Prevent future ponding after settling by allowing sufficient drainage angles.
   g. Pay particular attention to possible extreme settling and the problems that might occur given its new configuration.
   h. Make underground gutters to guide water off the front and away from the building.
   i. Cover it with flashing if it exits the ground.

Earth Tubes
1. Size 4 to 18 inches (4 to 46 centimeters) in diameter
2. Length 60 feet (18 meters) minimum. More like 100-200 feet (30-60 meters).
3. Must go downhill from the house at least a foot plus the diameter of the tube.
4. Must be kept relatively level (1/4 inch to the foot (2 cm/m) for drainage) in those places where convection power is to be MINIMIZED.
5. The greatest angle of grade must be in those areas where convection power is preferred.
6. At least TWO tubes must be used.
   a. One that enters the home at the highest point where air can be taken from.
   b. The other enters the home at the lowest point where air can come into the home.
7. Provide for condensation removal (drainage).
8. Provide for backfill settling so that the tubes will not be sheared off. (Backfill with gravel under the tubes.)
9. Provide bug screens.
10. A small umbrella should be provided over the tube if it is not under the main umbrella (about 8 feet wide, full length).
11. Do not "short out" the Storage Zone of the earth tubes by placing it too close to the interior walls so that conduction becomes a more prominent factor than the convection through the tubes.
12. Plastic tubes should work quite well, their R-value is small (given their thickness) and they can withstand the earth environment for a long time.

Internal Design
1. Light colored walls and ceilings to spread the heat around.
2. Medium colored floors so that they will be ever so slightly warmer than the ceiling, to help balance out stagnation.
3. Carpet SHOULD make little difference.
4. Allow for a free flow of air between the places where sunlight comes into the home and the conductive surfaces adjacent to the storage so heat can be transferred by convection.
5. Provide a place for the WARM air to go.
6. Provide a place for the COOL air to go.

Window Layout

1. Use moderately sized windows. Greater than the 10% required by law, and less than the usual passive solar recommendation. Probably about 25% to 30% of the equivalent floor area in glazing.
2. Do not localize the windows all on the south as if it were a regular passive solar building. Spread the windows out so that the timing of the heat input is spread out over the whole day.
3. At the same time (be careful) DO NOT severely reduce the conductive surface area, and thus the storage mass accessibility.

Adjustments

1. EXTERNAL shading devices that are ADJUSTABLE!
2. Earth tube shut-offs and one way doors.
3. Windows, floor vents, sky lights.
4. Provide for cross ventilation and, high and low vents also with earth tubes.

Monitoring

At least, monitor critical temperatures inside, outside and in the storage mass.

Waterproofing

- Insulation/watershed umbrella
- Gravity drainage.
- Do not allow hydrostatic pressure from water table.
- At least one layer of plastic as a VAPOR BARRIER.
- USE THE COMPLETE WATER CONTROL PROGRAM.

Appendix B

Conversion Tables
Multiply:

Linear Mesaure
    30.48 (Feet) = Centimeters
    .3048 (Feet) = Meters
    2.54 (Inches) = Centimeters

Area
    .09290 (Square Feet) = Square Meters

Volume
    .02831685 (Cubic Feet) = Cubic Meters
    7.4805 (Cubic Feet) = U.S. Gallons
    .76455 (Cubic Yards) = Cubic Meters
    3785.4 (U.S. Gallons) = Cubic Centimeters
    3.7854 (U.S. Gallons) = Liters

Mass
    1,016 (Tons) = Kilograms
    {2000 Pounds}

Heat
    251.99 (BTU) = Gram Calories (CAL)
    .25199 (BTU) = Kilocalories (KCAL)
    .000292875 (BTU) = Kilowatt-hours

R-Value
    .08065 (HR-FT2-EF/BTU/IN.) = HR-M2-EC/KCAL/CM
    {INCHES THICKNESS -->- CM THICKNESS }

Solar Energy

3.15 x 10-7 (TU/SQ. FT./HR) = KW/M2

Temperature Conversion

°C = (°F-32)/1.8

Bibliography

Out of the piles of publications put on the public market each year only a fraction contains that "one new item," that one really slick idea that makes the difference between doing something really neat or doing it half baked. Here is a list of some of the good ones I have found.

Earth Shelter Living. WEBCO Publishing Inc. (bimonthly)

Greery, Daniel. (1982). Solar Greenhouses: Underground. Blue Ridge Summit: Tab Books, Inc.

Mazria, Edward. (1979). The Passive Solar Energy Book. Emmaus: Rodale Press.

Mother Earth News. (bimonthly

Oehler, Mike. (1979). The $50 & Up Underground House Book. New York: Van Nostrand Reinhold Co.

Rodale's New Shelter. Emmaus: Rodale Press. (bimonthly)

Shelter Special. (1982). Mother Earth News.

Superintendent of Documents. The Uses of Earth Covered Buildings. Washington, DC: U.S. Government Printing Office.

The Underground Space Center, University Of Minnesota. (1979). Earth Sheltered Housing Design, Guidelines, Examples and References. New York: Van Nostrand Reinhold Co.

Wright, David. (1979). Natural Solar Architecture, a Passive Primer. New York: Van Nostrand Reinhold Co.

About the Author

John Hait began inventing at the age of ten, when he obtained his first Amateur Radio License. Following four years of electronics training in the U.S. Air Force, he returned to the University of Montana and the Missoula Technical Center. In 1981, he founded the Rocky Mountain Research Center as a nonprofit scientific research and educational corporation in Montana, its purpose being to advance these exciting new sciences, and teach others about them.

He has over 48 U.S. patents and patents pending covering nearly the entire foundation of photonic computing and fully photonic telecommunications. This work led him to discover the pseudorandomness of nature and from that, the fundamental mechanism of physics, Resonant Fields.

A prolific commercial inventor, his work spans a wide range of physics including secure electronics, high-speed 2048 bit encryption, HDTV, high-bandwidth radio and other photonic transmission systems, alternative energy production, water and gasohol distillation, wave, wind and water power... along with solar power that doesn't run down at sundown!

In 1979 he invented Passive Annual Heat Storage, a natural method of collecting heat in the summertime and storing it until winter.

An accomplished writer and public speaker, he completed his first book in 1983, "Passive Annual Heat Storage," which has sold world-wide. Then he wrote the book, "How to Recycle Scrap Metal into Electricity", all about Rust Power! Plus he wrote for numerous magazines including cover stories for Popular Science, Mother Earth News and the Computer Applications Journal.

Additional Information & Resources

For additional information and resources about Passive Annual Heat Storage, please visit our website at www.EarthShelters.com

PAHS DVD

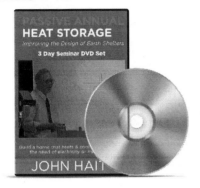

PAHS eBook

PAHS House Plans

PAHS Information Sheets

Made in the USA
Middletown, DE
20 August 2018